The Loch Ness Monster

by Stuart A. Kallen

ReferencePoint Press™

San Diego, CA

For more information, contact:
ReferencePoint Press, Inc.
PO Box 27779
San Diego, CA 92198
www.ReferencePointPress.com

Picture credits:
cover: Science Photo Library
AP Images: 6–7, 9, 26, 40, 43, 51, 58–59
Maury Aaseng: 12, 84
Fortean: 48, 67
Landov: 20, 69
Science Photo Library: 16–17, 23, 34, 80, 90–91

Series design and book layout:
Amy Stirnkorb

LIBRARY OF CONGRESS CATALOGING-IN-PUBLICATION DATA

Kallen, Stuart A., 1955-
The Loch Ness monster / by Stuart A Kallen.
  p. cm. -- (The mysterious & unknown series)
  Includes bibliographical references and index.

  ISBN-13: 978-1-60152-059-3 (hardback)
  ISBN-10: 1-60152-059-X (hardback)
  1. Loch Ness monster--Juvenile literature. I. Title.
  QL89.2.L6K35 2008

  001.944--dc22   2008021839

CONTENTS

FOREWORD

"Strange is our situation here upon earth."
—Albert Einstein

Since the beginning of recorded history, people have been perplexed, fascinated, and even terrified by events that defy explanation. While science has demystified many of these events, such as volcanic eruptions and lunar eclipses, some remain outside the scope of the provable. Do UFOs exist? Are people abducted by aliens? Can some people see into the future? These questions and many more continue to puzzle, intrigue, and confound despite the enormous advances of modern science and technology.

It is these questions, phenomena, and oddities that Reference-Point Press's *The Mysterious & Unknown* series is committed to exploring. Each volume examines historical and anecdotal evidence as well as the most recent theories surrounding the topic in debate. Fascinating primary source quotes from scientists, experts, and eyewitnesses as well as in-depth sidebars further inform the text. Full-color illustrations and photos add to each book's visual appeal. Finally, source notes, a bibliography, and a thorough index provide further reference and research support. Whether for research or the curious reader, *The Mysterious & Unknown* series is certain to satisfy those fascinated by the unexplained.

INTRODUCTION

The Legend of Nessie

More than 1,400 years ago an abbot named St. Adamnan wrote about an *aquatilis bestia*, or water beast, said to be living in a Scottish lake called Loch Ness. In the centuries that followed other writers referred to the creature as a leviathan, a water-horse, a dragon, a "loathy worme" (loathsome worm), and the Great Orm.

Witnesses say the Loch Ness monster is a humpbacked beast with flippers, a lengthy tail, and a horselike head atop a long sinewy neck. It might be a mythical sea serpent, a huge eel, a mutant dolphin, a humongous seal, or the last living dinosaur. Whatever it is, the creature refuses to die. Nessie's existence was first reported in the year A.D. 565. Unless modern witnesses are seeing the great-great-grandchild of an ancient lake beast, Nessie might be the oldest living organism on Earth. Or a family of monsters lives and breeds in Loch Ness. As with many mysteries, the questions raised

Did You Know?

The first eyewitness report of the Loch Ness monster was recorded in A.D. 565.

by this monster far outnumber the answers.

Today the loathsome worm thought to be living in Loch Ness is most commonly called a monster. This word derives from the Latin *monstrum*, meaning "omen." It is a term used to designate a thing that is rare and whose appearance is a warning of strange events to come. Little wonder then that whenever someone sees the Loch Ness monster in the cold Scottish lake

The ruins of Urquhart Castle are located on the shores of Loch Ness, in Scotland. The loch is 23 miles long and 754 feet deep.

strange events usually follow. For example, in June 2007, tourist Gordon Holmes shot some blurry video footage supposedly showing the Loch Ness monster bobbing in the water. When the video was shown on CBS, CNN, FOX, BBC, ABC, and NBC, excited reporters breathlessly inferred that this might be the real Loch Ness monster. Skeptics, however, pointed out that it was probably a small motorized toy boat.

The Last Living Dinosaur

Conflicting views over Loch Ness monster sightings have been making news for decades. And dedicated monster hunters have spent countless hours on hundreds of fruitless expeditions meant to track down the beast affectionately known as Nessie. Meanwhile, eyewitnesses, skeptics, the media, and the public have kept the legend alive. Perhaps this has to do with peoples' love of a good mystery. Or maybe it has to do with the millions of dollars tourists bring into the Loch Ness region every year. Whatever the case, a small but committed group of scientists and explorers remain adamant that something unusual lurks beneath the frigid waters of Loch Ness. And every year about half a dozen people claim to have seen the thing.

The Water Horse

Perhaps someday somebody will irrefutably prove that the Loch Ness monster is real. Until such time researchers will record each sighting of a hump, tail, head, or fin. And zoologists, writers, bloggers, and scientists will continue to theorize on the true nature of Nessie.

Intense speculation no doubt keeps public interest in the Loch Ness monster alive. Nothing demonstrates this better than the success of the 2007 film *The Water Horse* about a boy who finds a giant egg on the shores of Loch Ness. The egg hatches to reveal a Nessie-like creature which is raised by the boy before being turned loose in the loch. *The Water Horse* took in over $94 million worldwide, and critics were nearly unanimous in their praise for the picture. People liked the movie because it showed Nessie to be a little frightening but mostly benevolent. This may be why the Loch Ness legend has endured for so long. While people

Actor Alex Etel poses with a paper water horse, the star of the 2007 film The Water Horse, *about a boy who finds a giant egg on the shores of Loch Ness. The egg hatches to reveal a Nessie-like creature which is raised by the boy before being turned loose in the loch.*

like a good scary story, they do not want to be too alarmed. With the Loch Ness monster, they can have their beast in a form that is easy to enjoy and call it by a cute name like Nessie.

In a world where real-life horrors are everywhere, the beast of Loch Ness is a mystery monster people can live with. It is not a ravenous blood-drinking vampire or a deadly poltergeist but simply an awe-inspiring serpent that feeds on fish. And with its cartoonish face and clumsy body, the Great Orm brings smiles rather than tears to those who choose to believe in mythical creatures of the deep.

CHAPTER 1

Centuries of Sightings

In the year A.D. 565, an Irish poet and clergyman known as Columba of Iona left his homeland in Ireland and sailed east across the North Channel to Scotland. Columba, who was later given sainthood in the Catholic Church, was on a mission to convert the fearsome warrior tribes known as the Picts. The Picts, who lived in the central Scottish Highlands, were great artists who tattooed their own bodies extensively with plant-based ink. They also carved amazingly detailed pictures of animals into stone.

When Columba arrived in the Loch Ness region, he recognized all the animals in the Pict sculptures but one. This was a strange-looking beast with a long muzzle or beak, a spout atop its head, and flippers where its feet should have been. In this ancient age the Picts would never have known about animals native to Africa, but in later years scholars described this Pictish art as a swimming elephant. This picture, possibly 1,700 years old, still stands in a field near Loch Ness. It shows that the lake has long been home to unidentifiable aquatic creatures.

"A Great Roar and an Open Mouth"

It is unclear whether the Picts were carving a water creature they had actually seen. In ancient Scottish culture, huge, mythical animals have long been associated with bodies of water. It was believed that small streams, rushing rivers, and deep, cold lakes were home to water kelpies or water horses. These creatures had evil intentions and used supernatural powers to lure children onto their backs for rides. After the children clambered aboard the massive beasts they were dragged deep into the water to drown. The childrens' livers were said to wash ashore the next day.

It is unknown whether St. Columba knew of this legend, but about a century after his death in 597, St. Adamnan claimed Columba had a run-in with a real live water kelpie. The biography Adamnan wrote about Columba, *The Latin Life of the Great St. Columba*, includes a chapter called "Of the Driving Away of a Certain Water Monster by Virtue of the Prayer of a Holy Man," which contains the following story:

> [When] the holy man [St. Columba] was staying for some days in the Province of the Picts, he found it necessary to cross the River Ness. When he came to the bank, he sees some of the local people

Map of Loch Ness

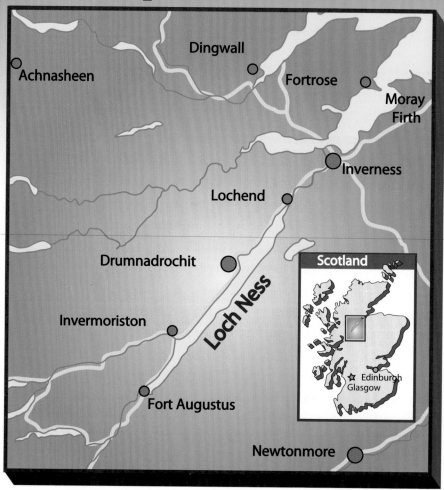

Source: Legend of Nessie, "About Loch Ness, Map of Loch Ness," 2008. www.nessie.co.uk.

burying an unfortunate fellow, whom—so those burying him claimed—some aquatic monster had shortly before snatched while he was swimming and viciously bitten. The corpse had been rescued by some boatmen armed with grappling hooks. The holy man orders one of his companions to swim out and bring over a [fishing boat] moored on the other side. Hearing and obeying the command, Lugne Mocumin without delay takes off his clothes except his loin cloth and casts himself into the water. But the monster perceiving the surface of the water disturbed by the swimmer suddenly comes up and moves towards him as he was crossing in the middle of the stream, and rushed up with a great roar and an open mouth.[1]

According to Adamnan, just as Mocumin was about to be attacked by the "fearsome beastie,"[2] Columba raised his hand to the sky and invoked the Lord. He commanded the beast to stop: "Go thou no further nor touch the man; go back at once."[3] The creature obeyed the holy man and made a hasty retreat as if it had been dragged off by ropes. Not only did St. Columba save the distressed stranger, this account stands as the first written record of a "fearsome beastie" in Loch Ness. And according to mountaineer and author Richard Frere in *Loch Ness*, "It was indeed a famous miracle and one which seekers after the True Monster, 1400 years later, would give their souls to see re-enacted."[4]

Whatever the veracity of St. Columba's tale, children growing up around the loch have been warned about playing too near the banks of Loch Ness. A persistent fear going back many generations still exists among locals that a great beastie might rise up and snatch the children.

Strange Goings On

Perhaps people around Loch Ness are superstitious because of the somewhat spooky atmosphere of the region. Even without the lake monster, on many days Loch Ness looks like the perfect environment to shoot a horror movie. The area is known for its dark, cloudy skies, towering waterfalls, stark craggy peaks, and thick pine forests. On the shores of the loch the ruins of the medieval Urquhart Castle, complete with a dungeon, adds to the mysterious ambiance. Describing the moody landscape, London journalist Percy Carter writes, "The Loch oppresses me. . . . Its surface, suggestive of its sinister depths, is as forbidding as anything I know. In this harsh landscape it is easy to think of strange goings on in the loch.[5]

Long before Carter wrote these words in the 1950s, people did indeed report strange goings-on. In 1871 an observer known as D. Mackenzie was crossing Loch Ness in a boat when he saw a monster that looked like an overturned rowboat with a log sticking up. The creature, apparently aware of Mackenzie's approach, suddenly sped off, churning up great waves.

Nessie was unseen again until 1885 when several people reported seeing an unidentifiable hump, tail, or head in the water. One of the observers, Roderick Matheson, said he saw the entire body of the beast, claiming it was "the biggest eel I ever saw in my life, [with a] neck like a horse."[6]

Matheson's description was one of several given in that era. The captain of a steamer that traveled daily between Inverness and Abriachan said the animal was a furry mammal with legs, not an eel, which is a type of fish. A traveler on the captain's steamer, however, described his Loch Ness monster as a salamander, which is an amphibian.

In the late 1880s H. J. Craig was fishing with his brother near the ruins of Urquhart Castle by the town of Drumnadrochit. Craig saw a huge serpent rise from the water, which sped off toward Inverness. The brothers were nearly hysterical from the sighting and shakily rowed their boat to shore. They were warned by their father not to tell anyone about the huge reptile they had seen in Loch Ness. The story eventually leaked out, but at that time locals were afraid to notify the outside world about their water monster for fear of ridicule.

By the 1890s, however, tales of the Loch Ness monster were starting to spread beyond the region. Stories about what was called the "horrible great beastie"[7] were reported in the *Glasgow Evening News* in Scotland and as far away as the Atlanta, Georgia, *Constitution*. Although it is unknown how the American newspaper knew of Nessie, the article was reportedly accompanied by a realistic drawing of the monster.

A Sharp Bark, Like a Dog

In the early years of the twentieth century Nessie sightings once again increased. In 1903 John MacLeod was fishing when he said he saw an animal 30 to 40 feet (9m to 12m) long lying motionless in a pool of water. The creature had a long tail and a head like an eel. Over the course of the next several years fishermen, travelers on the steamer, and the local postman described a creature similar to the one reported by Mackenzie, which appeared as an overturned rowboat with a loglike neck. One man who reported a sighting, James Cameron, was so shaken by the event that he

"The monster rushed up with a great roar and an open mouth."

—St. Adamnan writing in the seventh century about a great beast attacking a man swimming in Loch Ness.

This artwork depicts a Nessie-like creature coming ashore. Some stories about the creature claim it is a ferocious beast.

became fearful of walking alone along the road next to the loch.

Some in the community remained skeptical about the existence of the Loch Ness monster. However, a local paper began printing a column that contained sightings and speculations about the nature of the beast. Soon the area pubs and meeting halls were filled with talk of Nessie, and many residents kept binoculars handy in case they caught a glimpse of the beast during their daily travels by the loch.

One of the most detailed sightings of Nessie in the modern era, however, took place in the middle of the night in April 1923. Alfred Cruikshank of Banffshire said he was driving his Model T Ford around the loch at 3 A.M. when he had an encounter with the Loch Ness monster, which was crossing the road:

> My view of the Monster was: body, 10–12 feet long, 5 feet 6 inches to 7 feet in height, tail 10–12 feet. Colour, green-khaki resembling a frog, with cream coloured under-belly which trailed on the ground. It had four legs thick like an elephant's and had large webbed feet, in reality it looked [like] an enormous hippo, but [with an] arched back and long trailing tail, which was on the same level as the belly. . . . It gave a sharp bark, like a dog, as it disappeared over the road into the water.[8]

Ten years later a woman identified as Mrs. Thomas MacLennan claimed to have seen a different creature sunbathing near Urquhart Castle. Calling it the ugliest sight she ever saw, MacLennan described a beast with a fishlike body, woolly hair on its back, and short, thick legs with hooves like a pig's but larger.

Because the creature was up on a ledge high above the water, MacLennan said it must have "climbed like a monkey"[9] to get up there. She let out a cry when she saw the beast and startled it. The creature then slithered off the cliff on its stomach and fell into the water with a great splash. Describing this event, MacLennan said "It did not stand up like, say a cow. It kept its hind legs on the ground seal-wise. It seemed too heavy in the body for its own legs."[10]

Some time after MacLennan's sighting, a pilot was flying over Loch Ness when he said he saw a creature that resembled an alligator, only much larger, about 25 feet (7.6m) long and 4 feet (1.2m) wide. The airman, a member of the Royal Air Force (RAF), recommended placing a depth charge in Loch Ness which would kill Nessie on contact. This would provide positive proof of its existence. The idea was dismissed as cruel as well as impractical since it would endanger local boaters.

A Loathsome Sight

While random Nessie sightings made local headlines, the Loch Ness monster phenomenon as it is known today did not really begin until 1933. That year a new road was opened along the northern shore of Loch Ness that provided unobstructed views of the water. With easier public access to the lake shores, monster reports began appearing regularly in the papers. However, it was a driver on the loch's south shore that changed the nature of the Loch Ness region forever.

On July 22, London businessman George Spicer and his wife were driving near Whitefield when they said they saw a bizarre creature on the road. Spicer later described what he called the horrible abomination:

"Quote"

"The Loch oppresses me. . . . Its surface, suggestive of its sinister depths, is as forbidding as anything I know."

—London journalist Percy Carter, describing the bleak atmosphere of Loch Ness.

The remains of the medieval Urquhart Castle are on the shores of Loch Ness. The castle is now a tourist attraction.

First we saw an undulating sort of neck, a little thicker than an elephant's trunk. It did not move in the usual reptilian fashion but, with three arches

in its neck, it shot across the road until a ponder-
ous body about four feet high came into view. . . . It
has been a loathsome sight. . . . It was terrible. Its
color, so far as the body was concerned, could be
called a dark elephant grey. It looked like a huge
snail with a long neck.[11]

Mrs. Spicer later said the animal seemed to have an object
slung over its back, such as a deer or lamb carcass. She also said
the creature's neck moved up and down like the tracks of a rail-
road going over hilly terrain.

About a month after the sighting, George Spicer wrote a letter to the *Inverness Courier* describing the encounter. He asked
if anyone knew what the animal was and if anyone else had seen
it. The letter caused a stir in Inverness. On August 9 the paper
printed a headline asking if the Loch Ness monster was related
to an extinct marine reptile that had a large flat body, paddlelike
limbs, and a short tail: "Is It a Variant of the Plesiosaurus?"[12]

The plesiosaur lived about 65 million years ago during the Me-
sozoic era, and scientists doubted that any specimens could have
survived. However, the public was charmed by the idea that
their loch might hold what they thought of as the world's last
living dinosaur, and the sightings continued. In January 1934 a
21-year-old veterinary student named W. Arthur Grant claimed
to have nearly hit the beast with his motorcycle. While riding
on the north shore of the loch at one A.M., Grant saw a hefty
creature with front flippers. As he jammed on his brakes, the
thing bounded across the road and dived into Loch Ness. Unlike
Spicer's beast, Grant's monster had a head like a snake or eel
with oval eyes, a long neck, and dark brown skin.

Opposite
page:
This artist's
rendition
shows plesio-
saur diving
for food. The
plesiosaur
lived about
65 million
years ago,
and scientists
doubt that
any speci-
mens could
have sur-
vived. How-
ever, some
people who
have encoun-
tered Nessie
liken it to a
plesiosaur-
like creature.

An Ancient Sea Cow

Grant's sighting, along with the other recent reports, spawned a worldwide Loch Ness monster mania. Suddenly the British press was brimming with stories about Nessie sightings. Headlines read: "Monster's Color Mystery—Black, Creamy, or Speckled?" "Three People See Monster—Could Not Be a Boat," "Like a Giant Worm," and "Mystery Beast Believed to Be an Ancient Sea Cow."[13]

As fantastic sightings were reported as fact, experts began to weigh in on the issue. E.G. Boulenger, director of the aquarium at the London Zoo, said the Loch Ness monster sightings were a striking example of mass hallucinations. Another scientist, W.R. Pycraft, wrote in the *Illustrated London News* that the reports were simply a result of uneducated people viewing large seals for the first time.

The pronouncements of mass hallucinations and giant seals were quickly forgotten in November 1933 after Hugh Gray went on a photographic expedition around Loch Ness. Perched on a 30-foot cliff (9m) near Foyer with his camera pointed at the water, Gray claimed to have seen the round back and tail of an unknown animal bursting out of the water with a great arch of water spray. The photographer quickly took 5 pictures before the beast disappeared. Inexplicably, Gray left the film undeveloped for 3 weeks, and when it was printed, 4 of the photos were blank due to errors on the part of the cameraman. The one picture that did come out was extremely inconclusive. Gray's cheap box camera was unable to freeze the motion of whatever was moving through the water. Experts who examined the pictures said it could be a bottlenose whale, a shark, ship wreckage, or even a rotting tree trunk. Whatever it was, Gray's picture was published in the *Glasgow Daily Record* and was soon seen in newspapers across the globe.

The Surgeon's Photograph

Several months after Gray's picture was published, an amazing photo was taken by R. Kenneth Wilson, a London surgeon. Wilson was driving several miles beyond Invermoriston when he said he saw a disturbance in the loch about 500 feet (152m) from shore. After noticing a small head atop a thick neck rising out of the water, Wilson grabbed his camera and took four shots.

Wilson had the pictures developed immediately by a chemist in the next town. Two were blank but the third picture distinctly showed what appeared to be an unusual creature with a small, horselike head, two small nubs for horns, and a thick neck. Never before had such a clear picture been taken of what might be the loch's local water serpent. The fourth picture showed only the head of the creature as it sank beneath the water.

Wilson's third picture, called the "Surgeon's Photo," was promptly published in the *London Daily Mail* and soon appeared in dozens of other newspapers and magazines. While experts puzzled over the authenticity of the picture, Wilson was said to have a sterling reputation. At the time, friends said he would not risk his medical career by passing off phony photos of the Loch Ness monster.

As with Gray's photo, zoologists, biologists, and the untrained public all weighed in on the "Surgeon's Photo." The object in the picture was described variously as a diving otter, the dorsal fin of a killer whale (orca), and a freshwater diving bird such as a grebe, cormorant, or heron. But because the image resembled numerous earlier physical descriptions of the Loch Ness monster, many simply accepted the idea that the subject of the photo was the world's last plesiosaur.

Monster Seekers

The intense interest in the "Surgeon's Photo" helped sell newspapers as the story was picked up by the international press. By the summer of 1934, people from across the globe were pouring into the region hoping to see Nessie themselves. Suddenly the formerly desolate roads around Loch Ness were filled with hikers, bikers, and smoke-belching cars and buses. Industrious locals converted their homes into bed and breakfast hotels, while ship operators began conducting tours of the loch.

The publicity brought a spike in purported sightings. Many of these came from tourists referred to as "Monster Seekers" by local residents. Other reports came from those who were drawn to the loch by financial interests—the New York Zoo had offered the equivalent of a $75,000 reward to anyone who could capture Nessie alive. To counter the offer, a British carnival, the Bertram Mills Circus, offered $100,000. This sparked a local movement to protect the Loch Ness monster, and the chief constable of Inverness issued an order to prevent anyone from harassing or capturing the beast. The British Parliament even debated whether or not Nessie should be afforded official protection, but no law was ever enacted.

Throughout 1934 Nessie sightings were reported almost weekly. Some said the beast had one large hump, others said 2 or 3. One person reported seeing 9 humps, or possibly 2 Loch Ness monsters. Richard Horen clamed to have been less than 100 feet (30m) from the beast and watched it frolic in the water for 20 minutes. Others only saw Nessie for a few seconds or a few minutes at a distance of .25 miles (.4km) or .5 miles (.8km). The creature was viewed early in the morning, late at night, during

This image, taken by Hugh Gray in 1933, was published worldwide. The image was eventually revealed to be a hoax in 1994.

the middle of the day, and in rough waters, choppy waves, and calm, glasslike conditions. People said it was light brown, dark brown, black, gray, dark olive, and even orange. Fuzzy, grainy pictures were taken that showed objects that appeared to be logs, whales, turtles, and unidentifiable flotsam. However, the London press had moved on to political scandals and other sensational stories to sell papers. The Loch Ness monster eventually became old news.

Creature in Camouflage

Only the *Glasgow Herald* kept continual track of the Nessie sightings, and the newspaper tallied 51 between 1934 and 1956. However, by the mid-1930s, Nazi leader Adolf Hitler had become chancellor of Germany, and World War II was looming. With the outbreak of the war in 1939, lighthearted pursuits such as tracking the Loch Ness monster were replaced in Great Britain by the very real need to ensure the nation's survival. In the Loch Ness region, soldiers were keeping a sharp eye out for Nazi submarines and bombers rather than mutant dinosaurs.

Skeptics who do not believe in the existence of Nessie point out that during the war years, when Loch Ness was most heavily observed by soldiers, the beast was sighted far fewer times. Of course this was also a period when people were not taking vacations and many local men were away serving in the military. Nonetheless, one notable report occurred during this era. In June 1942 C.B. Farrell, a member of the Royal Observer Corps, was on watch at 5 A.M., searching the skies over Loch Ness for enemy bombers. Farrell noticed a disturbance in the water about 750 feet (280m) away from where he was standing. Peering through his high-quality, military-issue binoculars, the soldier says he distinctly saw a creature with a graceful neck about 4 feet (1.2m) long. It appeared to be feeding, and it slowly dipped its head down into the water, then raised it and shook it forcefully. After a few minutes, it disappeared into the water. Farrell claimed the beast was a dark olive color with brown circles. Why the creature would be camouflage colored remains unknown. Perhaps

Farrell's imagination played tricks on him after the Italian air force falsely claimed it bombed Loch Ness and killed the famous monster. Or the soldier, who had been on watch all night, simply imagined seeing the camouflage, if not the entire incident.

A Bulbous Body and Eight Legs

It is not unexpected that almost as soon as the war ended in 1945, Nessie sightings picked up again. Perhaps freed from the fear of Italian bombers, the creature emerged again in August 1946. At that time, its small horselike head and long neck popped out of the water and nearly knocked over a Mrs. Atkinson who was standing on the shore.

As the sightings continued throughout the early 1950s, a new method of monster detection was employed on Loch Ness. The technique of echo sounding or echolocation was first developed to help ships ascertain the depth of the seas. Like sonar, echo-sounding emits a beep which bounces off an object and returns to the machine. Operators are able to measure distance by tracking the time it takes the sound to reach an underwater object, echo off of it, and return to the ship. In 1954 the ship *Rival III* began using echo sounding in Loch Ness to chart the topography of the lake bottom. It soon discovered a mysterious object 480 feet (146m) under the surface. The recorded graph was analyzed by technicians who determined the object was not a school of fish. It seemed to be a large, solid animal. Although echo sounding cannot determine the exact shape of its target, experts say this reading showed something with a large, bulbous body and 8 legs. Because of the inexact nature of the primitive technology, the accuracy of this outcome could not be proved. Like eyewitness sightings of the time, it largely passed unnoticed.

Project Water Horse

By the late 1950s tales of the Loch Ness monster began attracting a new type of monster seeker to the region. These people were obsessed with Nessie and determined to find it. Aerospace engineer Tim Dinsdale was among this fanatical group. He had read an account of Nessie in a British magazine and it changed the course of his life.

In April 1960 Dinsdale drove from his home in Berkshire to Loch Ness with a borrowed 16mm movie camera and a telephoto lens. After six long days of pointing his camera at the loch, Dinsdale saw Nessie and began filming. He believed he was seeing a single specimen from a group of water monsters that lived in the loch, as he writes in *Project Water Horse*:

> [At] 9 A.M. I saw and filmed a member of the colony from a point high up on the southern shore. . . . I saw it very clearly, with the sunlight shining on it, and while viewing it, the Monster (for monster it was in size) came to life and surged away across the water, slowly submerging and then turning abruptly left, close to the far shore, and proceeding underwater for half a mile, trailing a great wake behind it. I shot about forty feet of black-and-white film of the animal, then later filmed a boat steering the same course, for comparison.[14]

QUOTE

"The Monster . . . came to life and surged away across the water, slowly submerging and then turning abruptly left . . . proceeding underwater for half a mile, trailing a great wake behind it."

—Engineer Tim Dinsdale's account of the creature he filmed with his movie camera in 1960.

Months after it was shot, Dinsdale's 4-minute film was re-leased to the press and shown on news programs throughout the world. Some who analyzed the film, however, believed the object had the dimensions, appearance, and speed of a rowboat powered by a small outboard motor. While believers saw what they said was proof of Nessie's existence, the film was largely dismissed by experts. In 1966, however, the controversy was once again in the news. Dinsdale's film was analyzed by the Joint Air Reconnaissance Intelligence Centre (JARIC), a branch of the British Royal Air Force. They concluded that the thing in the film was probably an animate object, that is, a living creature, moving at about 7 miles per hour (11kph). Dinsdale dedicated the rest of his life to proving the existence of the Loch Ness monster, writing 7 books about Nessie and conducting 56 expeditions, many of them solo. Before his death in 1987, Dinsdale said he briefly saw the head and neck of the beastie 2 more times.

Several of Dinsdale's expeditions were conducted with a group of London volunteers who had formed the Loch Ness Phenomenon Investigative Bureau in 1962. (The group later changed its name to the Loch Ness Investigation or LNI.)

The LNI was led by David James, a member of the British Parliament whose experience included naval service and exploration in Antarctica. Throughout the 1960s and 1970s, LNI studied the loch and its monster intensively. They compiled and analyzed 258 sighting reports and correlated them with weather and water conditions. They mounted 12 photographic expeditions with the hope of capturing a clear image of the beast. And the group even used psychological techniques to examine the mental health of Nessie spotters.

The LNI issued annual reports, hired freshwater biologists,

and put underwater cameras in place. Yet Nessie remained elusive. The monster has only been seen an average of 5 times annually since the 1970s, and little proof of its existence has been produced. That has not stopped twenty-first-century observers from reporting their sightings of the Loch Ness monster. And the general descriptions vary little from those made 50, 100, or even 1,500 years ago.

The reports continue. But legendary Nessie hunter Robert H. Rines does not think the beast will ever be seen again. Although he saw the creature gliding through the waters of Loch Ness in 1971, he thinks Nessie is dead. According to a report in the Scotland *Daily Record*, "the trail has since gone cold and Rines believes that Nessie may be . . . a victim of global warming."[15]

Not everyone supports Rines's theory. Some say Nessie is part of a dinosaur family that has survived for more than 65 million years. If true, it is doubtful that a spell of global warming could kill such a hardy beast.

For skeptics the answer to the Nessie mystery is not global warming but a proverb attributed to Ben Franklin: "Believe none of what you hear and half of what you see."[16] When it comes to monsters, beasties, and horrible abominations it might be a good idea for Nessie hunters to consider Franklin's advice and believe none of the stories told about the creature and only half of what they see sailing across the frigid loch waters.

CHAPTER 2

Searching for Nessie

E ver since St. Columba purportedly saw the Loch Ness monster in 565, Nessie sightings have been largely accidental. Most who reported seeing the beast were not looking for anything unusual—the monster simply surfaced at a time when they happened to be gazing at the water. And while scientists have weighed in with their opinions about Nessie since the late 1800s, it was not until the 1960s that scientific expeditions were mounted to actively hunt for the Loch Ness monster. But because of Nessie's elusive nature, these expeditions proved no one would become rich from finding the monster.

Any scientific success relies on accurate information that can be repeatedly proved. But the data surrounding Nessie is notoriously unreliable. The time and place of the sightings has been so random over the years that guessing when Nessie would appear in Scotland's biggest lake was nearly as impossible as predicting an earthquake. It would take time and money to hunt for the mythical monster. Boats and expensive equipment needed to be purchased and salaries and living expenses had to be paid to workers and researchers. And while positive proof of the Loch Ness monster might bring fame, there was little fortune to be gained to justify the expense. Even a definitive picture of Nessie might be worth only a few thousand dollars to the photographer who took it. Despite these obstacles, more than half a dozen large-scale expeditions were mounted between 1967 and 2001 to search for the Loch Ness monster.

"Consider Every Possible Explanation"

Researchers wanted to find answers to several unanswered questions. They asked if unusual, unexplained events were actually taking place in Loch Ness. If so, they wanted to know if the activities were caused by living creatures or inanimate objects, such as logs. If a living creature was the source, they wanted to find out what sort of animal it was. Only a clear photo or video—or the capture of a living specimen—would provide satisfactory answers.

The efforts of the monster hunters were limited only by time, money, and imagination. Their options included trying to capture Nessie with bait or live traps or dredge the lake with nets hoping to snag the beast. They could patrol the loch with airplanes or boats at regular intervals, using photographic equipment to document activity. Alternately, movie cameras could be set up around the perimeter of the loch, covering the water from every angle. In the days before digital cameras, the cost of film and film processing made this a very expensive option.

Did You Know?

More than half a dozen large-scale expeditions were mounted between 1967 and 2001 to search for the Loch Ness monster.

The most thorough way of exploring Loch Ness was the most costly. Expensive sonar equipment could record any objects swimming through the water. Like echo sounding, this electronic imaging technique uses sound waves and time measurement to detect unseen underwater objects. Sonar could be fixed in one place or operated from a patrol boat.

Sonar could be accompanied by underwater searches using small submarines and teams of scuba divers. Submerged cameras might also be used to gather images, but the heavy concentration of peat particles in the water severely limited visibility. However, underwater microphones, called hydrophones, could record unusual animal sounds.

Related underwater activities could include mapping the exact shape of the loch, including caves and other places Nessie might be hiding. A list of food sources, aquatic animals, and water temperatures would also aid in determining the exact perimeters of Nessie's world. Discussing the complicated technical aspects of such research, Roy P. Mackal, biochemist and member of the LNI, stated:

Opposite page: This is an artist's rendition of the Loch Ness monster. Loch Ness is 754 feet deep, leaving plenty of room for a plesiosaurus-like creature to thrive.

> We needed to consider every possible explanation and plan experiments to test every hypothesis. In practice this can never be done completely because of the limitations of time, money, and human resources. One, or at most a few, of the more probable hypotheses are generally pursued. In our case the most reasonable explanation for the observations in Loch Ness seemed to be animals, perhaps an unknown species. Our approach was designed to test this working hypothesis while we

The first monster-
hunting expedition
on Loch Ness in 1967
cost the equivalent
of $123,000.

remained conscious of the ever-present possibility that our initial assumption might be partially or entirely wrong.[17]

The Loch Ness Expedition

Mackal joined the Loch Ness Investigation in 1965. By 1967 the group had raised enough funds to begin the Loch Ness Expedition, the first scientific study of Nessie. Most of the $20,000 cost (equal to about $123,000 in 2008), came from Field Enterprises, publisher of two Chicago newspapers, the *Daily News* and the *Sun-Times*. Field also published the *World Book Encyclopedia* and saw the expedition as a way to further scientific research while helping to sell newspapers and books.

The LNI used Field's money to purchase a good boat that would operate in the loch's infamously rough waters. The group also began major photographic research. It bought 16mm movie cameras, 35mm still cameras, and powerful telephoto lenses, which were employed at several camera stations around the loch. Between May and October 1967, the stations were staffed by 150 volunteers who kept watch over the loch in good and bad weather for up to 18 hours a day.

With so many volunteers, a party atmosphere prevailed. Observers included local residents and those from the United States, Canada, Belgium, Sweden, Denmark, and New Zealand. The publicity surrounding this effort also attracted reporters from many countries, and the research received mostly positive press in newspapers and magazines as diverse as *Reader's Digest* and *Machine Design*.

What was considered the first photographic success of the Loch Ness Expedition occurred on June 13, 1967, when 17-year-old student Richard Raynor shot a sequence of 35mm photos showing the wake of an object moving through the water. The pictures were taken with a telephoto lens from an embankment 50 feet (15.2m) above the water. The disturbance, at a distance of about 1.25 miles (2km), does not reveal a neck, head, hump, or tail. However, experts from the Royal Air Force analyzing the shape and size of the wake determined that the object was moving about 10 miles per hour (16kph) and was 20 to 25 feet (6 to 7.6m) in length. Eyewitnesses said that they saw the creature's back moving just below the surface of the water. Discussing the photos, Mackal states:

> The films provide independent, objective evidence for unknown animate objects in Loch Ness. About these animals we learn something of speed, mode of movement, size, and configuration. . . . [We] seem to be dealing with a deep-dwelling aquatic animal that only occasionally shows a small portion of its anatomy at the surface. A photographer is going to have to be spectacularly lucky if we [are to learn] more about our monster from surface film or photos."[18]

The Sonar Net

In addition to Raynor's photos, the expedition produced 23 Nessie sightings similar in content to those given in earlier years. However, as winter approached, the expedition was forced to wind down. It started up again in 1968 with an additional $10,000 provided by Field. More cameras were purchased, providing the expedition with 90 percent coverage of Loch Ness. But the

efforts to photograph the loch did little to advance the goals of the expedition. It was believed that sonar might help locate Nessie, and the LNI decided to go to the source of sonar expertise to continue its research.

D. Gordon Tucker was the chairman of the Department of Electronic and Electrical Engineering at the University of Birmingham, England. He was one of the world's leading experts on sonar technology, and in the spring of 1968 Tucker wanted to test a new type of long-range sonar device. This machine would create a sonar "net" that would detect movement from anything that passed through it. The movements would be recorded on the screen of an oscilloscope, a small television-like device that displays sonar signals on a graph.

After being contacted by the LNI, Tucker agreed to test his sonar from Temple Pier on Loch Ness. The device would direct its acoustic signals toward the opposite shore, creating an electronic net. Because of the expense, however, the expedition could not pay for someone to watch the oscilloscope day and night. Therefore, a 16mm movie camera was employed to film the screen at 10-second intervals.

Through the use of echolocation, the sonar detected a moving object about 20 feet (6m) in length diving very quickly. Later, a group of such objects was detected. Because of the diving capacities it was determined that the creatures had to be non-air-breathers. But according to the "Loch Ness Investigation Annual Report for 1968," it was impossible to determine what the creatures were:

> Since the objects . . . are clearly comprised of animals, is it possible they could be fish? The high rate of ascent and descent makes it seem very unlikely,

and fishery biologists cannot . . . suggest what [species of] fish they might be. It is a temptation to suppose they must be the fabulous Loch Ness monsters, now observed for the first time in their underwater activities! The present data, while leaving this as a possibility, are quite inadequate to decide the matter. A great deal of investigation . . . is needed before definite conclusions can be drawn.[19]

The Yellow Submarine

Although the researchers had yet to provide irrefutable proof of the Loch Ness monster, interest in Nessie remained high. In 1969 a survey of worldwide inquiries to the *Encyclopedia Britannica* showed that questions about Nessie were nearly as numerous as those concerning the recent manned moon landing. However, expedition members were no closer to proof. As dedicated researcher Adrian Shine writes on the Loch Ness Project Web site, "In human terms, the evidence for unusual creatures in the loch was overwhelming, yet photographic surveillance on the most massive and protracted scale could not produce verification."[20]

After three years of work by the LNI, a new group of monster hunters took over in Loch Ness. Mackal joined with Dan Taylor, a former U.S. Navy submariner, on a project to get down into the water and have a look around. Taylor used his considerable knowledge to build his own small, one-person, yellow submarine, *Viperfish.* (It is rumored that the Beatles wrote the song "Yellow Submarine" after hearing about Taylor's vessel.) The *Viperfish* was equipped with sonar and two biopsy harpoons. These special harpoons would not kill the monster but were designed to gather tissue samples should Nessie appear.

"[We] seem to be dealing with a deep-dwelling aquatic animal that only occasionally shows a small portion of its anatomy at the surface."

—Biochemist Roy Mackal, describing the creature photographed by expedition volunteer Richard Raynor.

Dan Taylor, a former U.S. Navy submariner and Loch Ness monster researcher, mans his submarine that can go as far as 2,000 feet deep.

During the summer of 1970 Taylor made 45 dives in Loch Ness. However, the weather that year was particularly harsh, and the homemade submarine was plagued with problems. *Viperfish* broke down, got buried in the mud, and lost contact with researchers on the surface. Several times Mackal feared that Taylor was forever lost beneath the waves. Although he did manage to survive every dive, the *Viperfish* was never able to secure evidence of Nessie's existence. But Taylor never gave up his desire to find the monster. In 2001 he began work on a larger, more powerful vessel to explore Loch Ness. Tragically, the submariner died from complications of surgery in 2005 when the boat was only 75 percent complete.

Knocks, Clicks, and Turbulent Swishing

In late summer of 1970 Mackal launched another project, the "Big Expedition." This mission involved deploying a system of hydrophones throughout the loch that would allow researchers to conduct acoustic monitoring. In this manner they hoped to hear the calls produced by underwater creatures.

The five microphones were attached to tape recorders sealed inside large steel drums. These drums floated on the surface, anchored to the bottom of the loch. The hydrophones hung down below the drums on hundreds of feet of microphone cable. When underwater sounds were detected, the tape machines automatically started to record on rolls of magnetic tape.

Like Taylor's experiment, the researchers faced many problems. Large waves, high winds, and major storms limited access to the hydrophones. Some equipment came unmoored and was lost. However, in late October the tapes finally revealed some unusual sounds, described as bird-like chirps, knocks, clicks, and turbulent swishing. Mackal describes his impression when he first heard the noises:

> [The] clicking sounds . . . seemed to come from multiple sources rising and falling in intensity. Suddenly we realized that these were not mechanical sounds but calls—produced by living creatures in the water below. . . . [It] was an awesome feeling. Somewhere nearby were unseen animals calling to each other. . . . Minute after minute the calls continued to be recorded. At last we had it—an extended recording of calls from unknown animals in Loch Ness.[21]

"A Triangular Appendage"

Like the sonar evidence, Mackal's recordings defied analysis. But they still did not provide proof of Nessie. And the Big Expedition was not alone in generating weird but ultimately useless information in 1970. As Mackal was setting his hydrophones in the loch, other expeditions were taking place. One was sponsored by the Asahi Camera Company in Japan and the distillers of Black and White Scotch Whisky in London. With plenty of funding the expedition utilized divers, professional photographers, and sensitive infrared cameras for night photography. Meanwhile, aeronautical engineer Dinsdale was conducting his own photo surveillance of the loch.

While the press covered the various Loch Ness missions, the most interest was generated by an expedition conducted by Robert H. Rines, a Boston attorney and president of the Academy of Applied Science (AAS). Rines believed that Nessie was a member of the eel family that breathed underwater through it skin. This led him to develop a number of scented potions to be spread in the water like bait to attract the Loch Ness monster. Some of the attractants were classified as smelling like food but the one that received the attention from the press was the "sex lure," hormones extracted from salmon oil. This bait was applied to a mock monster made of plastic buoys and canvas. Although the dummy was meant to attract a love-struck monster, it disappeared beneath the water within a day.

The press reacted predictably to Rines's use of sex hormones, describing the idea in joking and mocking tones. However, the lure was part of a larger plan. The AAS had joined forces with the Massachusetts Institute of Technology (MIT) to combine sophisticated sonar and underwater photography for the first time.

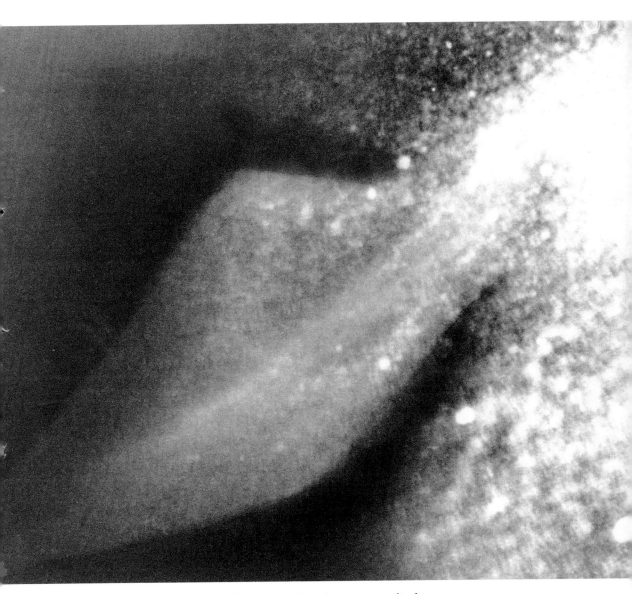

In 1972, Robert H. Rines, president of the Academy of Applied Science, released this image of what he claimed to be the flipper of the Loch Ness monster. The flipper could belong only to a very large creature, he said, since it was about 4 feet wide and 8 feet long.

The bait was meant to lure Nessie to the complex apparatus.

The newly developed side-scan sonar was attached to a camera and a strobe flash. When a moving object was detected by the sonar, it would trigger the underwater strobe-camera unit to take a series of pictures until the entity was out of range.

When the sonar-camera apparatus was put in place at Temple Pier on August 8, 1972, the results were immediate and dramatic. Within hours, a large object appeared on the oscilloscope which triggered the camera and strobe. The object was only about 100 to 150 feet (30.4 to 45.7m) from Temple Pier. When processed, the film revealed an unidentifiable object. Rines asked a friend at the Jet Propulsion Laboratory (JPL), a NASA research facility in Southern California, to enhance the photo using recently developed computer technology. After enhancement 2 of the photos appeared to reveal what the lab called a "triangular appendage appearing to contain 5 digits"[22] The appendage, or flipper, could belong only to a very large creature since it was about 4 feet (1.2m) wide and 8 feet (2.8m) long. According to H. Lyman of the New England Aquarium, the appendage "does not appear mammalian. General shape and form of flipper does not fit anything known today."[23]

Rines's photos were released to the world press and immediately created controversy. The 5 digits mentioned by the JPL were mysteriously missing from the photo, raising questions about how much the computer enhancement had changed the pictures. Some believed the pictures were altered to prove that Nessie was nearby.

Three years later Rines refined the photographic process, using brighter lights and a better camera placed 80 feet (24m) underwater. On June 20, 1975, the sonar triggered the camera several times, and the photos appeared to show in various shots the monster's head, its entire body, and finlike appendages. As with the 1972 pictures, the new photos were studied by the New England Aquarium and were said to confirm the existence of an unknown, animate creature in the loch. However, the peat-filled waters obscured the images and, once again, questions arose about the quality of the computer-enhanced pictures. Some wondered why the camera took crystal-clear pictures of eels and fish but only grainy, fuzzy images of the alleged monster.

The Ultimate Investigation

Despite the misgivings about the Rines photos, believers continued to point to them as proof of Nessie's existence. And like so many other disputed pieces of evidence concerning the monster, the photos only seemed to spur more expeditions in Loch Ness.

With worldwide interest in Nessie at an all-time high, perhaps it is not surprising that even respectable publications were prompted to act. In 1976 the AAS joined forces with the *New York Times*, which provided the equivalent of $72,000 to mount what was supposed to be the ultimate investigation of Loch Ness.

The researchers were outfitted with 35mm still cameras, a 16mm film camera nicknamed Old Faithful, and a video camera attached to television monitors. The cameras were attached to high-powered strobes. The mission statement explained the project: "When the operator sees a creature on the television monitor, he will immediately speed up the video tape recorder, and at the correct times press the button to take 35mm . . . pictures."[24] Portable videotape cameras had only recently come into use, so this was considered a high-tech expedition at the time.

The cameras were lowered into the waters of Urquhart Bay and held in place with anchors on the bottom and buoys on the water surface. One of the still cameras had a wide-angle lens which would give a more extensive view of the creature. Expedition member Dennis L. Meredith explained the benefit of this lens in *Search at Loch Ness:* "Should the beast swim between the camera and the surface, the wide-angle lens would capture its silhouette, perhaps its entire body. For the first time, the monster-hunters would know the shape of the entire creature, not of just a flipper or a head."[25]

With their cameras in place, the expedition took more than 108,000 pictures that summer. None, however, showed a Loch Ness monster. The crews could not even produce images of fish, which had been captured in profusion by previous expeditions. But the lack of fish was used to justify the failure of the mission. In 1976 the British Isles suffered a severe drought, and the salmon common to the loch had not spawned that year. Believers reasoned that a 2,500-pound beast (1,134kg) would need to eat about 250 pounds (113kg) of fish a day to survive. Without salmon to feed on, the beast was said to be keeping near the bottom of the deep loch where food was more abundant, far from the cameras.

Despite the lack of success, several purported Nessie sightings were reported in 1976. Two policemen said they saw the creature, as did a gas station attendant from Inverness. Unfortunately, a team of divers using a sophisticated underwater camera had no such luck. They were able, however, to take pictures of a woman's red high-heel shoe, an old teapot, and a saltshaker that had sunk to the bottom of Urquhart Bay.

Operation Deepscan

With the lack of success in the mid-1970s, the era of underwater photography drew to a close and the LNI decided to broaden its field of research. Instead of hunting for Nessie, the group began environmental studies of Loch Ness and nearby Loch Morar, which was half as big as Ness and said to harbor its own monsters. In 1979 the LNI changed its name to reflect this new interest and became "The Loch Ness and Morar Project." The following year researchers began to catalog the flora and fauna of the lochs, as well as their geological history. This was meant to help researchers understand the physical environment of the lochs and to develop theories about how giant animals might have survived there for centuries.

"QUOTE"

"It is a temptation to suppose they must be the fabulous Loch Ness monsters, now observed for the first time in their underwater activities!"

—A report by the Loch Ness Investigation speculating on the images recorded by a sonar net in 1968.

The Loch Ness and Morar Project also continued with sonar operations, using a 40-foot catamaran (12m) as a patrol boat. In doing so, the group found 40 unidentifiable objects in the early 1980s. However, these patrols also found that major sonar contacts were caused by large underwater waves, some 130 feet (40m) high. These huge waves are caused by rapid changes in water temperature at various depths. In summer, the warmer water layer near the surface is blown to the northern end of the loch by strong winds. This warm water mixes with the dense, cold water deep in the loch. When the wind slows in early autumn the warm water swishes back and forth, propelling ob-

On October 9 1987, 19 Operation Deepscan vessels equipped with echo sounders lined up side by side at Fort Augustus near one end of the loch. The vessels set out across the loch in a slow-moving line. The sonar detected one unidentified object, described as bigger than a shark but smaller than a whale. The object was gone before it could be investigated.

jects such as logs along the surface that take on the appearance of swimming animals. Meanwhile, huge underwater waves form in the layer between the cold and warm waters. While invisible at the surface, these waves can push massive objects such as log jams and rocks through the water. Researchers speculated that this underwater wave action caused the first unusual sonar contacts recorded by Tucker in 1968.

Undeterred by underwater waves, the Loch Ness and Morar Project continued their search for the elusive lake monster. In 1987 the group mounted Operation Deepscan, their most famous project to date. The idea was to assemble a flotilla that could beam a continuous sonar curtain through every square inch of the loch. Nessie would have nowhere to hide.

On October 9, 19 vessels equipped with Lowrance echo sounders lined up side by side at Fort Augustus near one end of the loch. The vessels set out across the loch in a slow-moving line. If unusual contacts were made, the boat *New Atlantis*, equipped with more sophisticated sonar, would move into position to track the movements.

The two-day Operation Deepscan mission was covered by hundreds of television crews and reporters from all over the world. Every hotel room around the loch was booked, and a party atmosphere surrounded the event. However, Operation Deepscan was not a stunning success. Three contacts were detected by the sonar curtain, but by the time the *New Atlantis* moved into place, the objects had departed.

One unidentified object, described as bigger than a shark but smaller than a whale, raised questions. The object disappeared after 2 minutes, and the following day 5 boats made a thorough search of the area to look for inanimate objects. Nothing was

*Opposite
page:
This frame
taken by an
underwater
camera in
1976 report-
edly shows
the head,
neck, and
body of the
Loch Ness
monster. The
sketch below
was added
to make the
frame clearer.*

found, and the object's identity remains a mystery. The blurry lines on the sonar reports did not create much interest in the press, and most journalists concluded that Operation Deepscan was a failure.

Project Urquhart

With morale hitting new lows among Nessie enthusiasts, it would be six years before another expedition would be mounted on Loch Ness. And the 1992–1993 Project Urquhart, named after the loch's ancient castle, would not be a full-blown monster hunt but an effort to once again closely study the environment of the loch.

Project Urquhart was organized by Nicholas Witchell, a BBC newscaster. A longtime Nessie buff, Witchell pulled together scientific researchers from London's Natural History Museum, the Freshwater Biological Association, the Simrad Marine Electronics company, and television's Discovery Channel.

At the beginning of the project, Simrad completed a thorough hydrographic survey of the loch. Using high-tech sonar and computers, the company mapped the exact depths and dimensions of Loch Ness by taking 7 million sonar measurements. In addition, sophisticated submersible crafts outfitted with video cameras captured images of debris, plants, and animals hidden beneath the waves. Trawlers collected fish and microscopic plankton, which were analyzed and cataloged according to species.

Although the researchers were not monster hunting, they did find unexplainable objects with their sonar. In July 1992 the sonar locked onto a large object for more than 2 minutes. The experts operating the sonar said it provided a much stronger signal than those given off by schools of fish they had been tracking. The

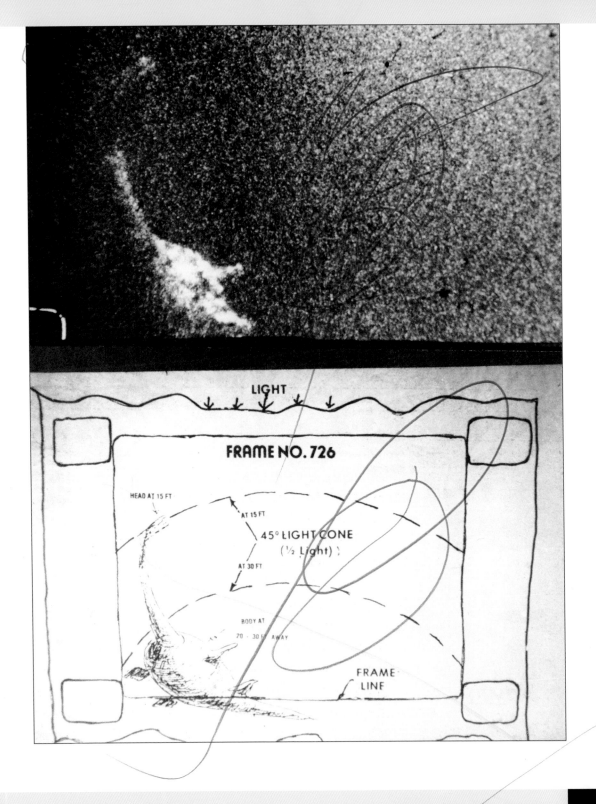

LIGHT

FRAME NO. 726

HEAD AT 15 FT

AT 15 FT

45° LIGHT CONE
(½ Light)

AT 30 FT

BODY AT
20 - 30 FT AWAY

FRAME
LINE

following year the crew found 4 "high value targets" in the middle of the loch, described by senior Simrad engineer Birnie Lees as "far too large to be one of the lochs' known fish."[26]

Once again, the sonar raised new questions but provided few answers. Project Urquhart never determined whether the loch contains enough fish to feed a 2,500-pound monster (1,133kg). It did show, however, that the loch held about 9 times more fish than previously believed.

Trapping Nessie

While amateur hunters continued to search for Nessie, interest in official expeditions remained low for many years. In April 2001, however, yet another monster hunt was under way when the Swedish Global Underwater Search Team (GUST) used advanced sonar equipment to search for the beast.

The GUST expedition was known as Operation Cleansweep, and it was controversial from the start. The leader of the team, Jan Sundberg, planned to search Loch Ness from one end to the other using a new model Simrad multibeam sonar. This type of search had been conducted many times and did not raise any objections. However, GUST proposed trapping the Loch Ness monster and collecting its DNA for analysis.

GUST planned to use a large eel trap, 23 feet (7m) long and

nearly 4 feet (1m) wide baited with eel to attract Nessie. Sundberg was not the first to propose such an idea. In 1933 a square cage the size of a small house was built to trap the monster. However, in the twenty-first century, biologists, researchers, and environmentalists strongly opposed the use of traps and DNA collection, fearing these techniques might harm the loch's famous beast.

Despite the protests, the project went forward and was filmed for a program called *Loch Ness Monster: Search for the Truth.* Once again, however, an expensive expedition proved little. The team observed a small, unidentified sonar disturbance on one occasion, and on another a sonar disturbance was captured on film.

With the failure of GUST to produce tangible evidence, the days of Loch Ness expeditions were over. With every inch of the loch mapped, explored, and cataloged by sonar, no one has conceived of a better way to find Nessie. The Loch Ness monster is either dead, never existed, or is so good at hiding that it will never be found.

CHAPTER 3

Phony Photos and Monster Hoaxes

Since the 1960s millions of dollars have been spent to search Loch Ness for its mysterious monster. Many of the Nessie hunters were driven by sheer fascination with the legendary creature. Others were motivated by the fame that a good photo or film of Nessie could bring. A third group of people slogging along the shores of Loch Ness wanted to perpetrate hoaxes. Some hoaxers started out as true believers, spent small fortunes to find Nessie, but ultimately failed. Driven by financial desperation or the desire to be taken seriously, they passed off bogus pictures and questionable information about the Loch Ness monster. And in doing so, they often found that no matter how ridiculous the scheme, a notable percentage of the public often believed it.

The perpetual interest in the Loch Ness monster was driven

by intense competition in the burgeoning British press to attract readers in the 1930s. In London alone, 5 daily newspapers coexisted, with circulation over 1 million copies a day. Large sensational headlines about frivolous topics like the Loch Ness monster helped sell papers. After the first photo of the Loch Ness monster, taken by Hugh Gray, was published in late 1933, a frenzy ensued in the press. Eager to scoop one another, several newspapers were directly involved in tracking the beast. This media participation was at the root of the first known Loch Ness monster hoax of the twentieth century.

Not a Legend but a Fact?

Editors at the *London Daily Mail* were furious that they had been scooped on the Gray photo by the much smaller *Glasgow Daily Record.* Determined not to let this happen again, the *Daily Mail* hired big-game hunter and filmmaker Marmaduke Wetherell to track down Nessie.

Wetherell and his assistant, Gustave Pauli, scoured the lake in a rented boat but could not produce evidence of the Loch Ness monster. However, shortly before Christmas 1933 the pair discovered some huge tracks leading into the loch. Pictures of the tracks were promptly run on the front page of the *Daily Mail* with a blaring headline that read: "MONSTER OF LOCH NESS IS NOT A LEGEND BUT A FACT."[27] In the article, Wetherell was quoted as saying that the footprints belonged to a 4-fingered beast, 20 feet (6m) long, with soft pads on its feet about 8 inches (20cm) across.

The big-game hunter carefully made plaster casts of the tracks, which were sent to experts at the British Museum several weeks after the story ran. However, museum biologists noted

"MONSTER OF LOCH NESS IS NOT A LEGEND BUT A FACT."

—Headline from the *London Daily Mail* published in December 1933.

immediately that the tracks had been made by a dried right foot of a hippopotamus. During this era, severed hippo feet were often used as umbrella stands and ash trays. Wetherell had been tricked by pranksters and was humiliated. Although he faded from public view, the end of the story was not known for another 60 years.

Big-game hunter and filmmaker Marmaduke Wetherell created the famous Surgeon's Photo of the Loch Ness monster using a toy boat and a sea serpent model.

Wetherell Gets His Revenge

In early April 1934, several months after the Wetherell controversy had died down, the *Daily Mail* was back in the monster business. The paper published the world-famous Surgeon's Photo of Nessie and attributed it to Colonel Robert Wilson. The photo doubtlessly helped increase tourism to the Loch Ness region and launched countless photo expeditions by monster seekers. However, the reason the picture is known as the Surgeon's Photo is that Wilson adamantly refused to have his name associated with it.

There have always been those who thought that Wilson's picture was fake, but they only had the photo print to study. No examinations were made of the photo negative until the *British Journal of Photography* analyzed it in 1984. Photo researcher Stewart Campbell scrutinized the Nessie image and concluded it could only have been made by an object about 3 feet (1m) long. Campbell believed it was a marine bird or otter, but it would be 10 more years before the truth was told.

In 1994 a 90-year-old man named Christian Spurling confessed that he helped create the phony Loch Ness monster picture. Spurling was the stepson of Marmaduke Wetherell, and he claimed his stepfather was eager to get even for the hippo-foot humiliation. Wetherall told his stepson, "We'll give them their monster."[28]

To create the monster, Wetherell and Spurling found a toy submarine and mounted a model of a sea serpent head on the back.

The object in the image was small, about 1 foot high (30cm) and 18 inches long (45cm). After the pictures of the phony monster were taken, Wetherell somehow managed to convince respectable citizen Wilson to take the photos to the *Daily Mail.* Thus, Wetherell found his revenge.

Another aspect of the Surgeon's Photo hoax received little mention over the years. Wilson said he took the pictures on April 1, 1934, April Fools' Day or All Fools' Day in Britain. However, the April Fools' timing of the photo was ignored by the public. On April 11, two days after the Surgeon's Photo was published, the *Daily Mail* reported, "Yesterday thousands of people visited the loch hoping to catch a glimpse of the monster. A line of motor cars traveled down both sides of the loch."[29]

Mysteriously Missing Film

In the 1930s, before the advent of television, still photographs of alleged lake creatures had the greatest public impact. However, monster seekers also used primitive movie cameras in hopes of capturing images of Nessie. And like some photographs, phony films could be made to fool the public.

The earliest movie of what was said to be the Loch Ness monster was taken in December 1933, around the time of the Gray photo. This 16mm film was shot by Malcolm Irvine and two assistants for Scottish Film Productions. Although some Nessie hunters spend years waiting for a glimpse of the beast, the image was captured suspiciously soon after the cameramen set up their equipment. According to Irvine, "We were so excited and elated when the Monster appeared that we had no time to think of the still cameras. What you see on the screen lasts less than a minute, but it . . . is something with two humps—that much is clear from the picture."[30]

The Loch Ness Monster

This carcass washed ashore in the Orkney Islands of Scotland in 1942. It was 25 feet long and weighed about 1,000 pounds. At first some people thought it was another Loch Ness creature, but it was later determined to be a basking shark carcass.

South African tourist
G.E. Taylor said he
shot a full-color,
16mm film of the
Loch Ness monster
in 1938, but it was
never shown to
the public.

Irvine described a beast traveling through the water at about 4 miles per hour (6.4kph), leaving a large wake of foam behind it. It is unknown, however, whether or not the cameraman was perpetrating a hoax, since he never showed the film to anyone. This would be the first in a series of purported Nessie movies that were never produced. Experts could only conclude that those claiming to possess such films were perpetrating hoaxes.

The Most Sensational Wildlife Film

It is unknown whether a retired physician known only as Dr. McRae was a prankster. McRae claimed to have shot a fantastic film of Nessie that has never been seen by the general public. Fishing writer F.W. "Ted" Holiday says he saw still photos taken from frames of the McRae movie and called it "the most sensational wildlife film of all time."[31]

McRae was on a photo expedition around Loch Ness in 1935. He says he saw the beast floating, sound asleep, on the surface of the water about 300 feet (91m) in the distance. The doctor said he pulled out his movie camera and filmed the motionless monster for 5 minutes. The footage is said to show a creature about 30 feet (9m) long, with 3 humps, an elongated neck with a bristly mane, a pointed head, narrow eyes, and small horns. Apparently the monster awakened and began writhing its neck, splashing, rolling, and turning in the water while waving its long scaly tail in the air.

McRae's film would prove the existence of Nessie beyond a doubt. But viewing it is a problem. McRae felt that showing the film would expose him to ridicule. As Holiday explains:

During the 1930's, the "Loch Ness Monster" was good for a quick laugh almost anywhere in the world. People absolutely refused to credit the beliefs of many Scottish persons of repute that such animals did exist and anyone who said they had seen a monster was treated almost like a mental defective. . . . [The] doctor probably felt a great distaste for the whole stupid business. He must have known quite well that those who had laughed the monster to scorn [such as reporters] would be the first to rush north in order to make commercial capital out of the sensation if the films were released. He was determined not to give the skeptics this satisfaction.[32]

As a result, McRae only showed the film to his closest friends and went so far as to create a secret trust that would control possession of the film after his death. The trust consisted of three men, and in 1969 the single survivor, Alistair Dallas, told Holiday he saw the movie many times. However, according to Dallas, the sensational wildlife film was allegedly locked in a London bank vault and, according to instructions in McRae's will, cannot be shown "until such time as the public takes such matters seriously."[33]

It remains unknown if McRae's trustees have any surviving children or grandchildren who might release the film in the future. However, the entire episode sounded dubious to Nessie investigator Alan Wilkins. In 1976 Wilkins interviewed Dallas who would not verify the existence of the trust and also admitted that he had no idea where the mysterious film might be stored.

"QUOTE"

"I am sure Nessie appeared as a result of my psychic powers."

—Self-described Wizard of the Western World Anthony "Doc" Shiels, commenting on photos he took of the Loch Ness monster.

Large and Rounded

So it went throughout the 1930s. Claims of irrefutable proof never materialized on film. Such was the case of South African tourist G.E. Taylor who said he shot a full-color, 16mm film of the monster in 1938 when color film was first introduced. Taylor described the creature in the three-minute film:

> Its body was large and rounded, with a tapering down to the neck which dipped under the water, becoming visible about 18 inches away, rising in an arch to about 6 inches above the water before dipping again. Where the arch re-entered the water it had every appearance one would associate with a head. The body showed about one foot above the water. Its colour was very dark.[34]

Taylor never produced his film but said he showed it to a few people. It was later described by author Maurice Burton in his book *The Elusive Monsters.* Burton said he saw Taylor's film many times but only reproduced its images as a series of handmade drawings in his book. Again, without proof it was hard for experts to accept that Taylor's film was anything but a hoax.

The Way the Water Works

Not all water-monster movies are locked in vaults or otherwise hidden away from the public. The most famous film of Nessie, shot by Dinsdale and shown on British television, is still considered proof positive that the Loch Ness monster is real. And in his 1961 best seller *Loch Ness Monster*, Dinsdale writes that he has observed many known animals, including sharks, dolphins, seals, crocodiles, and large sturgeons. However, he also states emphatically that the animal in the film does not resemble any of these. Concerning the authenticity of his images, he writes, "I am prepared to take an oath to the effect that the film is genuine and untouched, and that it portrays the back and wash of a large living creature of some variety unknown to me, and that I did examine it carefully through a pair of excellent . . . binoculars."[35]

Few skeptics doubt Dinsdale's sincerity, and he is not believed to be a hoaxer. But his film shows only an indistinct blob moving across the loch more than a mile away from the camera. The film was made as the sun was setting, and according to Dinsdale's own account, he was physically and mentally exhausted at the time of the sighting. He had driven over 1,000 miles (1,609km) on twisting, turning, 2-lane roads in the previous days and was sleeping only about 3 hours each night.

Skeptics believe Dinsdale's mind tricked him into seeing a monster that was not there. Despite the 1966 Royal Air Force analysis of the film that concluded Dinsdale was filming an animate object, tests were done later that contradicted the RAF. In 1999 British Nessie enthusiast Richard Carter analyzed the Dinsdale film and realized the image was undoubtedly made by a boat filmed under poor lighting conditions. To come to this conclusion, Carter re-created the scene in Dinsdale's film. Working with the same type of camera under similar lighting conditions, Carter's film of a small wooden boat looks remarkably like Dinsdale's purported image of the Loch Ness monster.

Carter states on The Nessie Hunters Web page that because of the loch's unusual natural qualities, it is easy for people to have

false perceptions about objects they see:

[While] out on the waters of Loch Ness [I] found out just how deceiving the waters of the Loch can be, with wind slicks darting across the water as though something was swimming just below the surface, and with the wash from boats still visible some 20 [minutes] after the boat has passed. At this point I realized how some of [the] sightings were genuine mistakes, by people not familiar with the way the water works.[36]

Carter continues to believe in the existence of the Loch Ness monster. But he also believes that Dinsdale deluded himself about the indistinct image in his film.

Skeptics who agree with Carter point out a rarely mentioned fact. Dinsdale's famous Nessie film was the second movie that the monster hunter shot that week. Two days earlier, Dinsdale had his first "monster" sighting in the exact same spot. As he did later, he pulled out his movie camera and began filming. However, he soon realized it was "no more than the wash and swirl of waves around a hidden shoal of rocks, caused by a sudden squall of wind!" After using up most of his movie film on the imagined beast he confessed that in his excitement he had been "fooled completely."[37] Dinsdale admits this was an embarrassing, amateurish mistake but claims it was not a factor when he made the second film two days later.

A Showman and a Charlatan

Despite the questions surrounding the film, a host of expeditions were inspired by Dinsdale's movie. And countless monster seekers traveled to Loch Ness to search for its elusive monster. Many of these people were sincere, but the motives of a few were open to question. Fifty-year-old former British army sniper Frank Searle generated the most controversy after he arrived in the region in 1970.

Searle sold 20 pictures said to be the Loch Ness monster to newspapers. These were taken in a five-year span after his arrival in the area. While skeptics could not believe Searle saw Nessie so many times in such a short period, the photos were believed to be genuine when they were made. But according to the *London Times Online* "most now believe [the pictures] were created using fence posts, logs, tarpaulins and old socks."[38]

Searle also sold copies of his photos from the Frank Searle Loch Ness Investigation unit set up in an old blue camping trailer parked on a lonely shore of the loch. However, Searle outraged dedicated Nessie hunters, especially after he passed off fake photos he constructed by pasting dinosaur drawings on pictures of the loch. One even showed Nessie and a UFO. As a result of this and other frauds, Searle was engaged in a long-running war of words with researcher Adrian Shine of the Loch Ness Investigation.

In 1983 the dispute intensified after the words "Shine con-man"[39] appeared in red spray paint on the ancient stone of Urquhart Castle. Shortly thereafter, the local community was shocked when Shine was injured by a gas bomb that exploded in his camp. Searle disappeared after the attack, and local monster hunters ran advertisements in British newspapers to track him down. But like the Loch Ness monster, no one could spot Searle for 22 years. Rumors said that he was treasure hunting in Cornwall, lecturing on monster hunting in the United States, or even lying dead at the bottom of Loch Ness. However, in 2005 a film crew making a documentary on Searle discovered that he had died a few weeks earlier, at age 84, in the Lancashire town of Fleetwood. In the obituary that followed this discovery, the *Times* called Searle "in equal measure a showman, a raconteur [storyteller], a hermit and a charlatan."[40]

The Wizard of the Western World

Searle was not the only self-styled showman living near Loch Ness. In 1977 Anthony "Doc" Shiels, who described himself as a wizard and "psychic entertainer,"[41] produced another iconic photo of Nessie. Clearly showing a motionless head and neck projecting out of the water, there are no ripples or splashes around the object. Few experts take the Shiels photo seriously, and skeptics refer to it as the Loch Ness Muppet because it so obviously resembles a puppet. However, Shiels insisted that he used supernatural means to attract the monster to his camera, telling *Tidbits* magazine, "I am sure Nessie appeared as a result of my psychic powers."[42]

After gaining a measure of fame with his odd Loch Ness Muppet photo Shiels claimed that a year earlier he had seen a sea

In 1977 Anthony "Doc" Shiels produced this image showing a motionless head and neck projecting out of the water, with no ripples or splashes around the object. Skeptics refer to it as the Loch Ness Muppet because it so obviously resembles a puppet.

"QUOTE"

"During the 1930's, the 'Loch Ness Monster' was good for a quick laugh almost anywhere in the world . . . and anyone who said they had seen a monster was treated almost like a mental defective."

—Fishing writer F.W. Holiday, discussing the public's reaction to movies allegedly showing Nessie.

serpent named Morgawr near the British town of Cornwall. Unlike Nessie, which lived in freshwater, Morgawr is said to be a saltwater serpent. In the introduction to the book *The Monster of Falmouth Bay* by A. Mawnan-Peller, Shiels listed other supernatural phenomena allegedly witnessed that year:

> 1976 was a very strange year indeed. . . . Not only did Morgawr perform, but there were reports of UFO sightings [at Loch Ness], "little people" [elves and fairies], witchcraft, mysterious sounds and smells, and the grotesque Owlman of Mawnan [a monstrous creature resembling a mix of 3 beings; an owl, a bear, and a man]. As the "Wizard of the Western World," I found myself at the epicenter of these happenings. . . . I enjoyed the experience.[43]

Hoax? Not a Hoax?

In later years, Loch Ness hoaxes seemed to belong more to the realm of practical jokers than wizards of the Western world. In May 2001 an unknown prankster dumped two conger eels in Loch Ness. These creatures can grow up to 10 feet (3m) in length and weigh over 60 pounds (27kg). However, they live in saltwater oceans, not freshwater lochs. Investigators came up with 2 theories about the appearance of the eels. They might have been put in place by hoaxers who planned to photograph them and pass the images off as the Loch Ness monster. Or else the jokers were simply hoping that others would see them and mistake them for little Nessies. Whatever the motive, the eels did not survive very long in the freshwater and the plan was a failure.

In July 2003 Gerald McSorley found an unusual fossil when he accidentally tripped and fell in the loch. He took the fossil to scientists at the National Museum of Scotland, who confirmed it was four perfectly preserved vertebrae of a plesiosaur. However, it was revealed that the vertebrae were encased in limestone typical of a saltwater environment and that they must have been planted in the loch as a hoax.

"QUOTE"

Two years later, a more complicated hoax was carried out by unknown pranksters. In July 2003 Scottish senior citizen Gerald McSorley found an unusual fossil when he accidentally tripped and fell in the loch. The elderly gentleman took the fossil to scientists at the National Museum of Scotland who confirmed it was 4 perfectly preserved vertebrae of a plesiosaur. This news excited monster hunters who claimed that the fossil was proof that Nessie or its relatives once lived in the loch. However, upon further examination, it was revealed that the vertebrae were encased in limestone typical of a saltwater environment. In addition, the fossil was said to be from the Jurassic period about 150 million years ago, while Loch Ness formed at the end of the last Ice Age about 10,000 years ago.

The credibility of the 67-year-old McSorley has never been challenged, and no one believes he is a hoaxer. But the facts concerning the find do not seem to make sense. Plesiosaur fossils are uncommon and therefore very expensive. The plesiosaur vertebrae that were found were worth about $500. If someone were to spend that much to perpetrate a hoax, investigators question why they would hide the specimen in the shallow water where McSorley found them. It would be more plausible for pranksters to leave the fossils on a busy beach were they would be sure to be discovered. Investigators also believe that if a person was trying to trick the public into thinking Nessie bones were found, they would probably plant something more recognizable than vertebrae, which are not readily identifiable. Finally, although it is not common knowledge, under the right environmental conditions a bone can become fossilized in a few decades. News reports stated the fossil was 150 million years old, but it could have been bones from the 1870s or even the 1970s.

Whatever the truth, even the scientists at the National Museum were unable to clearly identify the source of the bones. Not so McSorley, who told BBC News, "I have always believed in the Loch Ness monster, but this proves it for me. The resemblance between this and the sightings which have been made are so similar."[44]

The Loch Ness Imposter

The plesiosaur was the subject of another recent hoax, but this time the monster was easily proved to be an imposter. And although the phony Nessie was the source of more than 600 sighting reports, this beast was part of a very expensive publicity campaign for a television show.

In September 2004 British TV Channel Five spent over $220,000 to create an animatronic, or robotic, version of Nessie from polyurethane, rubber, and fiberglass. The beast, called Lucy, closely resembled a plesiosaur and was created over a period of 14 weeks by Crawley Creatures, an English special-effects company that helped create the model of Jabba the Hutt in *Star Wars: Return of the Jedi.* The monster was 16 feet (4.8m) high, weighed about 440 pounds (200kg), and was fitted with air tubes that moved its head, neck, and jaw. Guiding Lucy was a problem, however, and eventually several divers were needed to move the robot convincingly through the water.

For 2 weeks Lucy roamed the waters of Loch Ness, surfacing on occasion to startle tourists. Channel Five filmed peoples' reactions for the program *Loch Ness Monster: The Ultimate Experiment,* which was shown in August 2005. The robot was

seen near a campground and near Urquhart Castle and created a stir when it swam alongside a Royal Scot cruise ship that conducts tours of Loch Ness. Ronald Mackenzie, who runs the cruises, said: "The first time Channel Five put the monster in the loch even we were unaware of it, so we were pretty shocked."[45]

No Truth in the Tooth

Six months after Channel Five made headlines with their high-tech monster, a pair of American students attracted attention with a decidedly low-tech hoax. But like the TV station, the students were exploiting Nessie for their own commercial purposes.

The unnamed students were visiting Loch Ness for spring break when they said they found a huge tooth in the carcass of a deer. The students speculated that the tooth belonged to the Loch Ness monster, who had lost it while trying to capture the deer, which had escaped before dying. There was one problem, however. The students said they did not have the tooth, as it had been taken from them by a game warden. Nevertheless, they did have a few photographs, so they created a Web site (no longer active) to publicize the find with a description stating "It was a tooth—about 4 inches long, barbed and very sharp."[46] The Web site also demanded that Scottish authorities return their find.

Biologists who saw the pictures said the tooth was really an antler that belonged to a roe muntjac deer. Muntjacs are small deer, about 18 inches (46cm) high at the shoulder. Their antlers, which look like enormous teeth, break off when they battle with one another during mating season.

Eventually, the tooth story was traced to best-selling author Steve Alten. He created the Web site with the students as a publicity stunt to generate interest in his new horror novel *The Loch*.

People Still Want to Believe

Loch Ness frauds and hoaxes have occurred on a regular basis in the twenty-first century. While some pranksters have utilized high-tech robotics, others simply pass off phony photos on a Web site. But as the perpetrators understand, the mere mention of the Loch Ness monster is enough to generate intense interest from the press and the public. In summing up people's love of mysterious monsters, an unnamed Channel Five spokeswoman stated: "I think it shows that people still want to believe in the myth."[47]

Did You Know?

In 2005 two American students claimed that a muntjac deer antler was really a tooth from the Loch Ness monster.

CHAPTER 4

What Could It Be?

In the twenty-first century the Loch Ness monster is a major tourist attraction in Scotland. Families accompanied by infants and grandparents tour the loch in cruise ships searching for signs of Nessie. But not too many centuries ago, large bodies of water were fearful, dangerous places. In the ages before sonar, radar, and ship-to-shore communications, boats disappeared without a trace into the inky depths, and sailors were never seen again. While most shipwrecks were caused by winds, waves, storms, and icebergs, some defied explanation. Therefore, it was a common tradition in seafaring societies to blame baffling shipping disasters on water monsters that lurked beneath the surface.

Many of the legends concerned sea monsters such as the 9-headed hydra that played a large role in ancient Greek mythology. And back in the days when countless 100-ton blue whales

(90.7t) roamed the seas it was not hard for sailors to imagine even bigger leviathans hiding in the vast oceans. But ancient cultures also feared freshwater monsters that lived in lakes.

In Oregon the Nez Percé Indians described an aquatic horned monster 75 feet (22.8m) long with 7 humps along its spine. In Vermont the Iroquois had legends of a giant water serpent called Tatoskok, reputed to be the size of the Loch Ness monster. Closer to Scotland, ancient Irish sagas describe the Pooka and Piast, fearsome beasts that live in Lough Derg in Donegal. In Iceland ancient scribes wrote of the Skrimsl, a creature 46 feet (14m) long with a bulbous body.

The Pookas and Skrimsls represent a small percentage of lake monster legends. Throughout the world over 250 lakes are said to be home to large, unidentified creatures. And like the Loch Ness monster, these beasts continue to haunt the public waterways. They are sighted, photographed, filmed, and reported on by authorities. So many of these creatures are said to exist, in fact, that in 1955 French zoologist Bernard Heuvelmans coined a scientific term, cryptids, to label them. Cryptozoology translates from Greek as "the study of hidden animals." Cryptozoologists study cryptids like the Loch Ness monster which exist in myth and legend and through sketchy eyewitness accounts and questionable physical evidence.

"Nothing Is Impossible"

Cryptozoologists base their studies on fossil records, using examples of extinct prehistoric animals in order to investigate purportedly living cryptids. This tradition goes back to ancient times when primeval people based their belief in lake monsters on giant bones they found as they traveled through the countryside.

"No scientist on earth would say that the sea cannot contain the legendary sea serpent, however remote the possibility."

—Scottish journalist Philip Stalker, speaking about the Loch Ness monster connection to the plesiosaur.

As Virginia Morell explains on the *National Geographic* Web site, "In many instances, the legendary monsters are linked to actual fossils of marine reptiles that ruled the seas from about 250 million to 65 million years ago."[48] While no giant bones have been found on the shores of Loch Ness, the first skeletal remains of the long-necked, seagoing plesiosaur were discovered in Germany in 1823 and in England several years later. The find gripped the public imagination, and before long, people began seeing plesiosaur-like monsters along Scottish shores.

Some who believe in the existence of the Loch Ness monster say that plesiosaurs managed to survive for the past 65 million years. However, this flouts scientific logic since cold-blooded dinosaurs could not have survived in the frigid loch. But the theory was popularized throughout Great Britain in October 1933 by Scottish journalist Philip Stalker. Speaking about the Loch Ness monster connection to the plesiosaur on BBC radio, he said:

> Of course, you say, it's impossible. But nothing is impossible until experience has proved it to be so, and no scientist on earth would say that the sea cannot contain the legendary sea serpent, however remote the possibility, or that such a creature if in existence could not possibly find its way, perhaps before full growth, up the River Ness . . . and into the loch. . . . To my mind . . . the evidence available at present goes all the way to demonstrate the real existence of a creature much resembling in outline and structure the plesiosaurus of Mesozoic times.[49]

In later years, the plesiosaur link was again popularized by the Robert H. Rines photos taken in the early 1970s. The images so closely resemble the ancient marine creature that leading British naturalist Peter Scott asserted they were undoubtedly pictures of a modern plesiosaur. In 1975 Scott, who was the director of the LNI, gave Nessie the scientific name *Nessiteras rhombopteryx*, Greek for "the Ness monster with diamond-shaped fin."

While such a designation allowed Nessie to be registered as officially protected wildlife in Great Britain, critics pointed out that the letters of the name were also an anagram for "Monster hoax by Sir Peter S." Rines countered that by moving the letters around some more so they could spell out, "Yes, both pix are monsters. R." Whatever the truth, professional zoologists could not accept the scientific designation of the cryptid because the idea was too implausible to take seriously. Scott did use the photos to create an enduring painting of two Loch Ness monsters. They resemble swimming plesiosaurs with short stubby horns, bulbous bodies, and fins.

Despite the popularity of the plesiosaur concept, biologists say it is highly unlikely that a single creature could inhabit Loch Ness for more than 1,500 years. Unless it was a supernatural creature with the magical ability to defy aging, the beast would have to produce offspring. While legend has it that the water monster

lays a single egg before it dies, thereby continuing the species, the production of a fertile egg requires both a male and female animal. And biologists have pointed out that there would have to be at least 20 animals in a breeding herd for the species to have continued to reproduce over the years. If that were the case, bones and body parts of Loch Ness monsters would be littering the lake, and people would see living creatures frolicking in the waters on a regular basis.

If a huge herd of living leviathans did inhabit Loch Ness, they would starve to death because not enough fish are in the loch to feed them. And some people believe that is exactly what is happening. Steve Feltham spent nearly 20 years watching the loch for signs of Nessie. He believes that at one time as many as 30 monsters lived in Loch Ness, but they are now dying out from lack of food, which has caused them to stop reproducing. As he told reporter David Lister of the *Times Online:* "In the heyday of the sightings, back in the Sixties and Seventies, there were probably 20 or 30 of these animals but I believe that we're now down to the last half a dozen."[50]

Eels and Seals

The plesiosaur theory is among the most popular among Loch Ness monster enthusiasts like Feltham. Other observers, however, believe the lake monster is related to various living species. Some say Nessie is an eel, others believe it is a seal.

The eel theory has been around for many centuries, and giant eels were first mentioned in print by Timothy Pont in 1724: "The men of the Countrey aleadges and perswades others that the said Eels [in Loch Ness] are as big as an horse with one an Incredible length. It is likely to be true in respect that none of the countrey-men dare hazard themselves in a boat to slay the Eels."[51]

It is undoubtedly true that giant eels live in Loch Ness, and sightings of eels 10 to 16 feet (3m to 4.8m) long have been reported. While many reports of the Loch Ness monster describe a creature twice that size, it could be possible that an extraordinarily large, thick-bodied eel inhabits the loch. This type of eel, when described by local loch residents is often called a "horse" eel like the one mentioned by Pont. This description might refer to the creature's horselike head or the mane that is sometimes said to grow on Nessie's neck. However, no such thing as a horse eel exists, and if such a creature did exist it would be as rare as the Loch Ness monster. And it is doubtful that any other type of eel would be mistaken for the water beast. While swimming eels make humps that fit the description of Nessie, eels do not stick their heads up out of the water. In addition, no humongous eel has ever been found in Loch Ness, and the conger eel, the largest of the species, is only about a quarter of the size ascribed to Nessie.

Seals are much larger creatures and, like Nessie, are known to frolic in the waves, move quickly through the water, and sun themselves on shore. They also have the dark brown to shiny black color ascribed to the Loch Ness monster. Therefore, some believe that Nessie is simply an enormous seal that has grown to an unusually large size by eating the abundant salmon in the lake. As Mackal writes, the "elephant seal would be adequately large to account for a conservatively sized Loch Ness monster. Further, the [chilly] temperature of the loch would be comfortable for pinnipeds [seals, sea lions, or walruses]."[52]

This elephant seal lounges in the sun in Northern California. Some people believe elephant seals might have been mistaken for the mysterious creature over the years.

The problem with this theory is that seals frequently leave the water to sun themselves and breed. If a pinniped of huge proportions lived in the loch, there would likely be hundreds of photographs of the creature.

"I Would Bet My Shirt"

Widely accepted theories of seals and eels are dismissed by some of the colorful individuals who have conducted independent investigations of Loch Ness. Holiday is one such researcher, and he has developed his own unique theories about the lake beast.

Holiday claims to have seen the Loch Ness monster in 1962, and he said the creature was black, glistening, rounded, and 40 to 45 feet (12m to 13.7m) long. This would make it 3 to 4 times bigger than the largest seal. After viewing the monster, Holiday developed a theory based on an unusual fossil discovered 4 years earlier in Illinois by Frank Tully. The fossil, named *Tullimonstrum gregarium,* or Tully's Monster, was a small worm that lived 300 million years ago. According to Holiday, the Tully Monster's shape resembled the Loch Ness monster so closely that the 2 creatures had to be related. In *The Great Orm of Loch Ness* Holiday describes the fossil as having a bizarre appearance:

> It had an elongated body shaped like a submarine and at the front end was a slender swanlike neck topped by a tiny head with tooth-studded jaws. The powerful tail carried lateral fins. Across the creature's chest was a sort of bar which extended outwards from the torso and on the two

extremities were strange organs, thick and oval in section, which resembled stout flippers.[53]

The only problem with the Tully Monster, thought to be a distant relative of both the octopus and the garden slug, is that the fossil was only a few inches long. But Holiday speculated that the creature had grown into a Great Orm over the millennia and was likely responsible for dragon sightings throughout the Middle Ages as well as the Loch Ness monster. While Holiday's theory seemed far-fetched to many, he was convinced that the two monsters were linked:

> Tully's monster . . . firmly demonstrated that worm-like animals with the appearance of a plesiosaurus did once exist. . . . In dealing with the Orm it became possible to argue a rational case with actual specimens available for reference. . . . No-one knows whether the Orm of Loch Ness is a form of *Tullimonstrum;* but, talking most unscientifically, I would bet my shirt that it is."[54]

After many years of staring out into the waters of Loch Ness waiting for the monster to reappear, Holiday began connecting the Great Orm to the dragons and serpents that represent evil in the Bible. And he compared descriptions of biblical dragons with those of the Loch Ness monster. According to the American Monsters Web site, this led Holiday to believe that "the animals in the loch weren't really animals at all, but supernatural projections stemming from malevolent individuals who had decided to dabble in the dark arts."[55] In other words, wicked magicians were casting spells to create psychic visions that caused people to hallucinate the Loch Ness monster. This unusual theory led Holiday to write several books linking black magic and even UFOs with the lake monster. In order to stop the evil, he paired up with the Reverend Donald Omand in 1973 to exorcise the beast from Loch Ness. The BBC filmed the event and doubtlessly helped Holiday sell books. However, sightings of the Loch Ness monster continued after the exorcism, and Holiday died an untimely death in 1979 at the age of 59.

"Every Lake Has Its Kelpie"

Holiday was not the only person looking to ancient legends to find answers to the Loch Ness monster phenomena. The ancient Picts made carvings of water horses called kelpies more than 15 centuries ago, and some today continue to believe that the Loch Ness monster is a kelpie.

Kelpies look like beautiful horses and were often seen standing on the shores of Scotland's lochs and rivers. According to Scottish legend, kelpies are supernatural creatures with magical shape-shifting powers. They can appear as horses, sea serpents, cows, or even handsome young men with dark eyes and lake weeds in their hair. In 1812 the Reverend Patrick Graham wrote of these mythical beasts in *Sketches of Perthshire:* "Every lake has its Kelpie, or Water-horse, often seen by the shepherd, as he sat in a summer's evening upon the brow of a rock, dashing along the surface of the deep, or browsing on the pasture-ground upon its verge."[56] Unwitting young shepherds who try to climb on the kelpie become trapped on the animal's back and are devoured

Does the Loch Ness Monster Exist?

In June of 2007, 72 percent of people who responded to a posted question on the Atlas Forum Web site did not believe there is any type of monster in the Loch Ness.

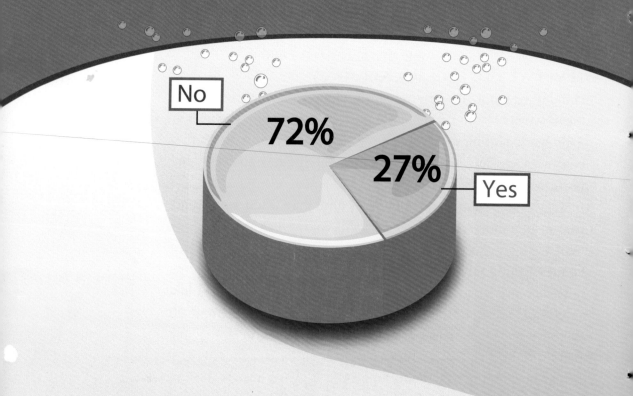

No
72%
27%
Yes

Source: Atlas Forum, "Does the Loch Ness Monster Exist?" June 1, 2007. www.uselectionatlas.org.

after the creature dives under the water.

Highland history is rich with accounts of the water kelpies behaving badly. In 1773 Doctor Samuel Johnson related a story in which a young girl was devoured by a wild beast, described as a sea-horse. The girl's father set a trap for the beast, throwing a sow upon a great fire. When the sea-horse was drawn to the smell of the roasting pig, the man killed the creature with a red-hot poker. Several decades later, a kelpie was blamed for the drowning deaths of a party of children who were attacked while crossing the loch. Even in the twentieth century fears of the killer kelpie remained. An unnamed author in *Bradford Antiquities* magazine described the kelpie in 1903 as a "fabulous goblin . . . a sprite that demands at least one life annually."[57]

Even as the article was published, physical descriptions of kelpies were undergoing revision. During this era Great Britain was experiencing dinosaur mania as the public became intensely interested in the discovery of prehistoric bones. What was once described as a horselike creature was now seen as a type of dinosaur, such as the plesiosaur.

Fermenting Logs?

Ancient legends aside, the list of possible animals that might have mutated into the Loch Ness monster is long and varied. In 1933 Rupert T. Gould, a highly respected lieutenant commander in the Royal Navy and author of several books on unexplained phenomena, compiled a list of possible Nessie candidates. The list included a monstrous newt, aquatic birds, otters, porpoises, turtles, tortoises, crocodiles, whales, and fish such as sturgeon, sunfish, shark, and ray. However, each possible creature was eliminated for one reason or another. Then in 2006 Neil Clark, curator of paleontology at the Hunterian Museum in Glasgow, suggested that Nessie was simply a swimming elephant. The creature was said to have run away from a traveling circus that was passing through the area in 1933. After the pachyderm's escape dozens of monster sightings were reported.

Clark's theory, like the others, has been dismissed by those who conclude the purported lake monster is not a living creature at all. Instead the skeptics say sightings are based on people mistaking natural occurrences such as wind, waves, and lake vegetation for a giant water beast.

Maurice Burton, a zoologist for the British Natural History Museum, once believed in the Loch Ness monster but became a skeptic in later years. In the 1950s Burton speculated the beast was a type of giant eel. Several years later he wrote an article saying Nessie was a relative of the plesiosaur or possibly a giant mutant turtle with no shell. However, after concluding an unproductive eight-day expedition on the loch in 1960, Burton became a nonbeliever. The following year he wrote the book *Elusive Monster* to debunk the popular theories about Nessie's animal nature.

Burton concluded that the Loch Ness monster was in reality rotting mats of leaves, lake weeds, and other organic debris. These were suddenly raised to the surface by gases given off during decomposition.

Burton's book was severely criticized by Nessie enthusiasts. They pointed to a 1903 Royal Geographical Society expedition on the loch that showed that the cold acidic waters prevent rapid decomposition of vegetable material. Leaves and weeds contained in the lake fall to the bottom and dissolve into powder. Therefore, no giant mats of matter exist, and if they did, they would not generate gases.

Although his theory was disproved, Burton remained convinced that the Loch Ness monster was fermenting plant matter. In 1982 he wrote a series of articles for *New Scientist* claiming that logs of Scots pine would occasionally rise swiftly to the surface of the loch. This was due to the high levels of resin sealed in the wood. As the resin decayed, gas built up in sealed bubbles within the log. When the pressure became too great, the bubbles would explode and propel the log through the water, causing it to dramatically shoot up into the air. According to Burton, the logs with their branch stumps closely resemble descriptions of Nessie.

Once again, believers criticized Burton's theory. Several lochs in the Highlands region contain rotting pine logs. However, no one has ever seen monsters swimming across them.

Roilings and Eruptions

While Loch Ness is not the only lake with pine forests on its shores, it does have some unique natural features. The loch is very long and its shores are relatively straight. Scientists say this causes an unusual water event called a seiche.

Seiches were discovered in 1890 on Lake Geneva in Switzerland, and the word roughly means "to sway back and forth" in the Swiss French dialect. On Loch Ness, seiches are caused by a steady wind that blows from northeast to southwest directly across the surface of the water. This causes waves to be blown to one end of the loch before the wind temporarily dies down and the water reverts to its natural level. The movement of the wa-

Did You Know?

Unusual standing waves called seiches are caused by the steady wind that blows across the surface of Loch Ness.

ter causes oscillations that make the water slosh back and forth. This movement has been compared with the motion of the water when a person gets out of a full bathtub. Sometimes this action will cause what is called a standing wave or a stationary wave. This phenomenon is a wave that rises above the surface of the water but does not move in the manner of a normal wave. The rolled, humped appearance could be mistaken for the back of a water beast by viewers standing hundreds of feet away.

Even if a standing wave is not created, seiches can still fool observers. Many eyewitness reports about Nessie describe a large commotion in the water with foaming and oddly moving waves. On the "Phenomenon at Loch Ness" Web page, geologist Andrew Alden describes how seiches produce rolling waves that might cause these conditions:

> Once started, seiches can continue for more than a week, [and create] hidden internal waves that affect the dense layers of cold water at the lake bottom. Interactions with the bottom topography and surface winds, not to mention wave interferences, are all capable of causing roilings and eruptions in the water. So there's a viable theory . . . not just for Nessie, but for the "lake monsters" documented in large cold lakes around the world.[58]

Underground Roaring and Shaking

Seiches can also be caused by earthquakes, even ones that occur hundreds of miles away. For example, a major earthquake in Lisbon, Portugal, in 1755 caused a large seiche on Loch Ness.

And earthquakes have also occurred directly under the lake. In
2001 Italian geologist Luigi Piccardi pointed out that most of the
Nessie sightings take place on the
northernmost part of the loch, directly over the Great Glen earthquake fault, which runs the entire length of Loch Ness. Piccardi
says the earliest monster sighting by Irish monk St. Columba in
the sixth century happened little
more than mile from where a major earthquake took place in 1901.

Piccardi says the energy released by the seismic event could
produce waves that look like vivid low humps cresting on the
surface of the water. And even minor earthquakes, too small for
people to notice, can release explosive bubbles of gas trapped
beneath the loch. This concentrated energy can cause frothing
and roiling on the surface. Commenting on this phenomenon to
the *Irish Times*, Piccardi stated: "Veneration of places like Loch
Ness may have been a result of people seeing unusual natural
phenomena there. These may have been gas and flame emissions,
underground roaring, shaking and the rupture of the ground."[59]

Like most Nessie theories, Piccardi's is discredited by believers like Gary Campbell, president of the Official Loch Ness Monster Fan Club. Campbell describes why the commotion caused
by quakes could not be mistaken for Nessie: "Over the last five or
six years that we've been recording sightings, none of them have

This illustration shows Nessie swimming in the shallow waters near Urquhart Castle. Today Web cams have been installed around the loch so if there is a monster, the public might one day see photographic evidence.

been of the bubble variety. Everybody has seen something solid so I don't know how an earthquake can be used to explain a solid hump or a solid headed Nessie."[60]

Boats or Beasts?

While earthquake experts and believers weigh in with their theories, the most reasonable explanation for the Nessie sightings might be the simplest. For centuries all manner of watercraft have crisscrossed Loch Ness, and since the mid-nineteenth century these craft have been powered by various types of engines. Moving boats produce wakes, which are said to create strange effects in the loch similar to seiches.

Boats traveling down the center of the narrow Loch Ness generate a wake that hits both shores simultaneously. Once they ricochet off the shores, the waves travel back and crash into one another in the middle of the loch. This action might create a standing humplike wave that is higher than the original wake created by the boat. And by the time this unusual wave is created the boat will have long passed from view. This leaves the impression that the water motion is independent from the boat.

The famous Dinsdale movie of the Loch Ness monster, which mostly shows unexplained wave actions, is instructive in this case. After shooting what many continue to believe is Nessie swimming through the water, Dinsdale turned off his camera for a few minutes. Then he moved it over and filmed a boat crossing Loch Ness. For some, this is enough proof that Dinsdale's monster was a boat, not a beast.

A Pragmatic Age

With so many theories and so few facts, the identity of the Loch Ness monster might never be confirmed. And in recent years the elusive Nessie has made research even more difficult. Only 2 sightings were reported in 2007 compared with dozens per year in the 1960s and 1970s. And despite the ubiquity of cell-phone cameras, digital video recorders, and even Webcams installed around the loch, no one has managed to produce a good image of the bashful Loch Ness monster.

Some say the water beast was killed by global warming or pollution; others say it is hiding from the ever-increasing number of boats on the lake. Nessie veteran Andrian Shine has another answer: People are simply too realistic in modern times to believe in mythical animals. As he told the *Times Online*, "I think we live in a more pragmatic age, and that people are becoming more aware of the sort of illusions that can occur on water."[61]

NOTES

Chapter 1: Centuries of Sightings

1. Quoted in Peter Costello, *In Search of Lake Monsters*. New York: Coward, McCann & Geoghegan, 1974, p. 25.
2. Quoted in Roy P. Mackal, *The Monster of Loch Ness*. Chicago: Swallow, 1976, p. 8.
3. Quoted in Mackal, *The Monster of Loch Ness*, p. 9.
4. Richard Frere, *Loch Ness*. London: John Murray, 1988, p. 35.
5. Quoted in Ronald Binns, *The Loch Ness Mystery Solved*. New York: Prometheus, 1984, p. 87.
6. Quoted in The Legend of Nessie, "The Evidence," 2007. www.nessie.co.uk.
7. Quoted in Costello, *In Search of Lake Monsters*, p. 28.
8. Quoted in Gerald S. Snyder, *Is There a Loch Ness Monster?* New York: Julian Messner, 1977, pp. 65–66.
9. Quoted in Costello, *In Search of Lake Monsters*, p. 35.
10. Quoted in Costello, *In Search of Lake Monsters*, p. 36.
11. Quoted in Snyder, *Is There a Loch Ness Monster?* pp. 66–67.
12. Quoted in Costello, *In Search of Lake Monsters*, p. 33.
13. Quoted in Snyder, *Is There a Loch Ness Monster?* p. 69.
14. Tim Dinsdale, *Project Water Horse*. London: Routledge & Kegan Paul, 1975, p. 3.
15. Quoted in Bob Dow, "Veteran Loch Ness Monster Hunter Gives Up," *Daily Record* (Glasgow), February 13, 2008. www.dailyrecord.co.uk.
16. Quoted in Think Exist.com, "Ben Franklin Quotes," 2006. http://thinkexist.com.

Chapter 2: Searching for Nessie

17. Mackal, *The Monster of Loch Ness*, p. 25.

18. Mackal, *The Monster of Loch Ness*, pp. 121–22.

19. Loch Ness Project Archive, "Loch Ness Investigation Annual Report 1968," 2000. www.lochnessproject.org.

20. Adrian Shine, "Loch Ness Timeline," Loch Ness Project Archive, 2000. www.lochnessproject.org.

21. Mackal, *The Monster of Loch Ness*, p. 77.

22. Quoted in Binns, *The Loch Ness Mystery Solved*, p. 154.

23. Quoted in Mackal, *The Monster of Loch Ness*, p. 111.

24. Quoted in Snyder, *Is There a Loch Ness Monster?* p. 146.

25. Dennis L. Meredith, *Search at Loch Ness.* New York: Quadrangle, 1977, p. 45.

26. Quoted in Legend of Nessie, "Searching for Nessie," April 20, 2008. www.nessie.co.uk.

Chapter 3: Phony Photos and Monster Hoaxes

27. Quoted in Binns, *The Loch Ness Mystery Solved*, p. 28.

28. Quoted in *Famous Pictures Magazine*, "Loch Ness," May 13, 2007. www.famouspictures.org.

29. Quoted in Binns, *The Loch Ness Mystery Solved*, p. 98.

30. Quoted in The Frasers, "Loch Ness Video Film Evidence," April 1999. www.thefrasers.com.

31. F.W. Holiday, *The Great Orm of Loch Ness.* New York: Norton, 1969, p. 114.

32. Holiday, *The Great Orm of Loch Ness*, p. 115.

33. Quoted in The Frasers, "Loch Ness Video Film Evidence."

34. Quoted in Costello, *In Search of Lake Monsters*, p. 72.

35. Tim Dinsdale, *Loch Ness Monster.* London: Routledge & Kegan Paul, 1961, p. 103.

36. Richard Carter, "The Nessie Hunters," The Frasers, April 1999. www.thefrasers.com.

37. Quoted in Binns, *The Loch Ness Mystery Solved*, p. 114.

38. *Times Online*, "Frank Searle: Territorial Hunter of the Loch Ness Monster, Who Produced Twenty Startling

Photographs of the Creature," May 30, 2005. www.timesonline.co.uk.

39. Quoted in *Times Online*, "Frank Searle."

40. *Times Online*, "Frank Searle."

41. Quoted in Binns, *The Loch Ness Mystery Solved*, p. 106.

42. Quoted in Binns, *The Loch Ness Mystery Solved*, p. 106.

43. Quoted in A. Mawnan-Peller, "The Monster of Falmouth Bay," Centre for Fortean Zoology, 2008. www.cfz.org.uk.

44. Quoted in Jordan P. Niednagel, "The Bones of Loch Ness," True Authority.com, April 27, 2008. www.trueauthority.com.

45. Quoted in *Daily Mail*, "It's the Loch Ness Impostor," August 17, 2005. www.dailymail.co.uk.

46. Quoted in Ron Strom, "Loch Ness Monster's Tooth Found?" World Net Daily, www.worldnetdaily.com.

47. Quoted in *Daily Mail*, "It's the Loch Ness Impostor."

Chapter 4: What Could It Be?

48. Virginia Morell, "Sea Monsters," *National Geographic*, December 2005. http://science.nationalgeographic.com.

49. Quoted in Binns, *The Loch Ness Mystery Solved*, p. 25.

50. Quoted in David Lister, "Has Scepticism Done for the Loch Ness Monster?" *Times Online*, September 29, 2007. www.timesonline.co.uk.

51. Quoted in Holiday, *The Great Orm of Loch Ness*, p. 94.

52. Mackal, *The Monster of Loch Ness*, p. 136.

53. Holiday, *The Great Orm of Loch Ness*, p. 140.

54. Holiday, *The Great Orm of Loch Ness*, pp. 143–44.

55. American Monsters, "Pioneers," 2008. www.americanmonsters.com.

56. Quoted in Scotland's Culture, "Kelpies," February 1, 2008. www.nessie.co.uk.

57. Quoted in Costello, *In Search of*

Lake Monsters, p. 132.

58. Andrew Alden, "Phenomenon at Loch Ness," About.com, April 29, 2008. http://geology.about.com.

59. Quoted in Unknown Country, "Latest Nessie Skeptic: It Really IS Hot Air!" July 9, 2001. www.unknowncountry.com.

60. Quoted in Unknown Country, "Latest Nessie Skeptic."

61. Quoted in Lister, "Has Scepticism Done for the Loch Ness Monster?"

FOR FURTHER RESEARCH

Books

Tim Dinsdale, *Project Water Horse.* London: Routledge & Kegan Paul, 1975. An older book worth reading, written by one of the premier Loch Ness monster hunters with details on the author's long expeditions on the Scottish lake, told with excitement and longing.

Judith Herbst, *Monsters.* Minneapolis: Lerner, 2005. Discusses various monster beliefs and legends, including those surrounding Bigfoot, the Loch Ness monster, the Swamp Thing, and Mothman.

Gary Jeffrey, *The Loch Ness Monster and Other Lake Mysteries.* New York: Rosen, 2006. An exploration of mysterious lake creatures, including the Loch Ness monster, the Lake Champlain monster, and South Bay Bessie.

Nick Redfern and Andy Roberts, *Strange Secrets: Real Government Files on the Unknown.* New York: Paraview, 2003. Explores a variety of subjects contained in secret government files concerning such topics as the Loch Ness monster, UFOs, and vampire legends.

Terri Sievert, *The Loch Ness Monster.* Mankato, MN: Capstone, 2005. Describes the history, sightings, and search for the Loch Ness monster.

Thomas Streissguth, *The Loch Ness Monster.* San Diego: Lucent, 2002. This book covers the views of skeptics and believers, leaving the reader to decide whether or not the Loch Ness monster is real.

Web Sites

The Legend of Nessie (www.nessie. co.uk). This site claims to be the official Web site of the Loch Ness monster and features hundreds of pages of info about Nessie, including photos, pictures, information about Loch Ness, and a link to the *Loch Ness Times.*

The Loch Ness and Morar Project, (www.lochnessproject.org). The most scientific source on Nessie, run by Adrian Shine of the Loch Ness Investigation. This site contains detailed information about

Loch Ness expeditions, many photos, and links to archival documents from the past 50 years.

Loch Ness Monster (www.youtube.com/results?search_query=loch+ness+monster&search_type=). This You Tube page has dozens of Loch Ness monster video clips from the realistic to the ridiculous and includes commercials, hoaxes, and movie outtakes featuring Nessie.

Museum of Hoaxes: Loch Ness Monster Hoaxes (www.museumofhoaxes.com/hoax/Hoaxipedia/Loch_Ness_Monster_Hoaxes). A very informative site with text written by Alex Boese, phony photos, fake fossils, and other hoaxes concerning the Loch Ness monster.

Nessie on the Net! (www.nessie.co.uk/htm/searching_for_nessie/urquhart.html). A live computer cam on Loch Ness with views of the water and Castle Urquhart.

Nessie's Grotto (www.simegen.com/writers/nessie/index.html). Lois June Wickstrom and Jean Lorrah maintain this entertaining site with links to Nessie lore, Nessie science, Nessie fun, and the latest Nessie sightings, which include recent photos.

DVD

Jay Russell, director, *The Water Horse: Legend of the Deep*, Sony, 2007. The story of a young boy who discovers the egg of the Loch Ness monster during the World War II era and befriends the beast after it hatches and grows into a full-size beast.

INDEX

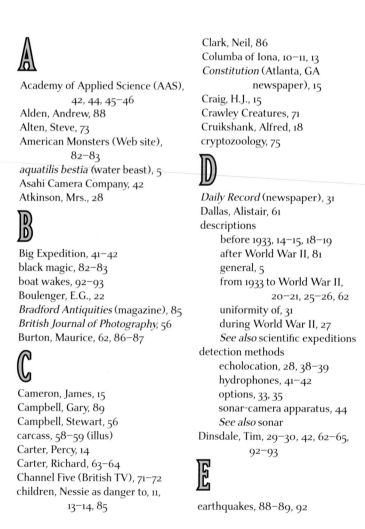

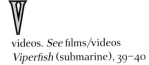

About the Author

Stuart A. Kallen is a prolific author who has written more than 250 nonfiction books for children and young adults over the past 20 years. His books have covered countless aspects of human history, culture, and science, from the building of the pyramids to the music of the twenty-first century. Some of his recent titles include *History of World Music, Romantic Art,* and *Women of the Civil Rights Movement.* Kallen is also an accomplished singer-songwriter and guitarist in San Diego, California.